HOLY GRAVITY

FEARING GOD FROM THE INSIDE OUT

LAURA JACKSON

Copyright © 2023 Laura Jackson

All rights reserved. No part of this book may be used or reproduced by any means, graphic, electronic, or mechanical, including photocopying, recording, taping or by any information storage retrieval system without the written permission of the author except in the case of brief quotations embodied in critical articles and reviews.

This book is a work of non-fiction. Unless otherwise noted, the author and the publisher make no explicit guarantees as to the accuracy of the information contained in this book and in some cases, names of people and places have been altered to protect their privacy.

WestBow Press books may be ordered through booksellers or by contacting:

WestBow Press
A Division of Thomas Nelson & Zondervan
1663 Liberty Drive
Bloomington, IN 47403
www.westbowpress.com
844-714-3454

Because of the dynamic nature of the Internet, any web addresses or links contained in this book may have changed since publication and may no longer be valid. The views expressed in this work are solely those of the author and do not necessarily reflect the views of the publisher, and the publisher hereby disclaims any responsibility for them.

Any people depicted in stock imagery provided by Getty Images are models, and such images are being used for illustrative purposes only. Certain stock imagery © Getty Images.

All Scripture quotations are taken from The Holy Bible, English Standard Version® (ESV®), Copyright © 2001 by Crossway, a publishing ministry of Good News Publishers. All rights reserved.

Scripture quotations are from the ESV Bible unless noted otherwise.

Other translations used are NIV, NASB, and NKJV.

ISBN: 978-1-9736-9897-5 (sc)
ISBN: 978-1-9736-9898-2 (hc)
ISBN: 978-1-9736-9896-8 (e)

Library of Congress Control Number: 2023909653

Print information available on the last page.

WestBow Press rev. date: 06/29/2023

CONTENTS

Acknowledgment		ix
Preface		xi
Introduction		xiii

Part I. Understanding the Fear of God

1	The Mystery of Fearing God	1
2	The Significance of Holiness	7
3	Knowing God	12
4	Two Fears	16
5	The Fearless	21
6	The Right Fear Among Wrong Fears	25

Part II. The Gospel and the Fear of God

7	The Weight of Sin	30
8	The Significance of God Revealed	34
9	Salvation and Judgment	39
10	Necessary Change	44
11	Forgiveness, Repentance, and Reconciliation	50

Part III. Wisdom and the Fear of God

12	The Beginning of Wisdom	58
13	The Significance of Scripture	64
14	Discernment	71
15	Self-Awareness	77
16	Prayer	82

Part IV. Love and the Fear of God

17	Love and Fear	89
18	The Significance of Love	94
19	A Heart that Fears	99
20	The Greatest Commandment	104
21	Second Chances	109

Part V. Obedience and the Fear of God

22	The Whole Duty of Man	117
23	The Significance of the Law	122
24	Confronting Our Disobedience	128
25	Obedience with Sincerity	134
26	The Fruit of Faith	140

Part VI. Suffering and the Fear of God

27	Revealing Fears	147
28	The Significance of Trust	153
29	The Good Gift of Suffering	159
30	Weak and Broken Vessels	164
31	Our Worship as Living Sacrifices	169

Conclusion   177

For Julia and Barnabas and the next generation,
As you live in a time filled with all kinds of fears,
may your lives be consumed by only One.

"Holiness, as taught in the Scriptures, is not based upon knowledge on our part. Rather, it is based upon the resurrected Christ indwelling us and changing us into His likeness." A. W. Tozer

ACKNOWLEDGMENT

To thank God with my words here seems like an incredible understatement. I thought many times while writing this book that it is my thank you to the Lord. My gratitude for His grace and mercy will never be enough, but thankfully, I have forever to demonstrate it. He has placed wonderful people in my life who have played important roles in making this book. My husband, Aaron, has sharpened and softened me as we have grown in love for each other and the Lord. I would not be who I am today without him; therefore, this book would not be here. Joseph Northcut has been a mentor to my husband in ministry and, in recent years, to me in this endeavor. His feedback and faithful encouragement propelled me forward throughout the writing and publishing process. I connected with Rebecca Dawson at my favorite copy place. She became a quick friend through her role as my book editor. I am grateful for her expertise, as her suggestions and corrections improved the book's quality and readability, which I pray will also improve its impact. Thank you to the many others who read chapters, offered feedback, and encouraged me along the way. God used you to shape this book into what it is today. And to the people who came into my life for a season, those who came and stayed, and those whose lives I invited myself into: thank you for the experiences we shared. The Lord worked in my life through you; again, this book would not be what it is without you.

PREFACE

My grief over the state of our world and what I believe to be the Holy Spirit's prompting led me to write what you hold in your hand. Besides writing an "award-winning" story in fourth grade and journaling through my teen and young adult years, I never thought much about writing. Writing for others was certainly not something I planned to do. But God has a beautiful and mysterious way of leading us to the good purposes He has for us. He often uses the giftings and desires He has given us, the places we have come from, and the experiences we have had to accomplish those good purposes.

I grew up in ministry in many ways. My parents were missionaries in West Africa during my childhood, serving with a worldwide missions organization my whole life. As a youth and young adult, I loved serving my church and participating in many local and international opportunities to serve others and share the love of Christ with them. Currently, I enjoy building relationships with people in my community through various ministries, raising my two children, and supporting my husband, who serves in full-time vocational ministry.

The years my husband and I have served the Lord by serving His people in our particular context have impressed upon us the great significance and privilege we have as individuals to serve one another with whatever God has given us wherever He has placed us. Whether we have time, talent or skill, passion, materials, or any spiritual gift, God means for us to use them to honor Him and benefit others, and we certainly reap blessings in the process. We have been tangential recipients of God's gifts He has given others, and we love being able to share our gifts too. I consider the time spent writing this book, the trials faced before, during, and after writing it, the passion for following through with it, and the content to all be gifts from God. They are not meant merely to teach and grow me but hopefully gifts that He will use to teach and grow His Church.

I feel it's important to share with you that I sat with the manuscript for this book for almost two years after writing it. During the season of writing and waiting for the next steps, my husband and I faced some challenging trials. My suffering exposed my weaknesses in the very area this book addresses. As I learned and wrote about the fear of the Lord, the Holy Spirit painfully revealed areas in my life tainted by so many other fears. He was training me to apply what He was teaching me on deeper levels, and the training continues today. My prayer is that this book will do the same for you.

Trials are hard for us, and that's the point. They test our knowledge by whether we apply it under pressure; that application being faith or trust in God which works in visible ways in our lives. Most of us would agree that life has been challenging these last several years, testing us in ways we may never have imagined. But what if these tests have been given by God to train us to fear Him? Tests that aren't meant to scare us into submission but to draw us near with His love. I know suffering doesn't seem like it can come from a loving God, but what if the trials in our lives serve to reveal God Himself? Could He be exposing the gaps in our knowledge of Him? Is He helping us learn who we are in light of who He is (and visa versa)? Is He turning us from sin and increasing our understanding of what it means to fear Him? From the moment I started writing this book, one question has called out from my heart: How might we be different, and how might the world look if, by God's grace, we learned and increasingly applied what it means to fear the Lord?

Laura Jackson

INTRODUCTION

"Who will not fear, O Lord, and glorify your name? For you alone are holy. All nations will come and worship you, for your righteous acts have been revealed." Revelation 15:4

"There is only one relationship that matters, and that is your personal relationship to a personal Redeemer and Lord. Let everything else go, but maintain that at all costs, and God will fulfill His purpose through your life." Oswald Chambers[1]

We need gravity. Its presence affects our lives, world, and universe every moment of every day. Interestingly, we can list its effects, like attracting all things with mass or energy to one another, giving weight to physical objects, or grounding us, without ever seeing it. Although we can't see gravity, we cannot deny its existence. Gravity affects everything around us, including ourselves.

On Earth, we experience the advantages of this invisible reality but venture away, and gravity's effects lessen their impact. As a result, we lose its benefits. The sensation of weightlessness may be a fun experience and we may escape some painful consequences of gravity, like dropped mugs on toes but the dangers far outweigh the fun. Leaving gravity doesn't only mean losing its benefits and escaping its consequences; without the protection of a spacesuit, it means certain death. Escaping the minor consequences doesn't seem as advantageous when confronted with that truth. Even to a lesser extreme, with a spacesuit perfectly tailored for an astronaut's body, scientific studies show they can lose up to 10% of bone density during six months in space. The reason for that loss is because our bones support our bodies against gravity. Without gravity, our bones can't serve their purpose so they weaken and deteriorate. Just as our bones need gravity, our souls do too. With it, we can thrive; without it, we die.

---

[1] Chambers, Oswald. 2015. *My Utmost for His Highest: The Classic Daily Devotional.* Barbour Publishing.

The Distance from Gravity

Our world is on a dangerous path. It has been for centuries, but it seems to be flying at lightspeed in the wrong direction: away from spiritual gravity. Keeping a good distance from gravity may seem pleasant to the unknowing heart, but it offers no benefits and only hopeless "freedom." If we're honest with ourselves, we know there is no satisfaction in weightless living and our flighty pursuits. We know we were made for gravity, but we cannot make our way to it on our own. And other people can't get us there, no matter how great their efforts.

Despite this, we still run to people and things to try to solve the ever-increasing problems in our world. In practical ways, they can relieve some of the pain we experience, but the relief doesn't last forever. Another problem comes up, and we struggle again. Even with all the experts and professionals promoting ways to improve our lives, our world flounders in chaos. There is more hate, rebellion, hypocrisy, self-gratification, and more self-everything. Why do we find ourselves worse off in our efforts to improve ourselves? I would argue it is because we are using the world's methods to try to solve an outside-of-this-world problem.

Our human efforts to ground ourselves with purpose will never work because the answer, holy gravity, cannot be found in a weightless environment. Only power outside of our sinful flesh, the power of God Himself, can ground us in holy gravity and change us as God intended us to be.

Our Need for Holy Gravity

Our souls were made for holy gravity. Holy gravity affects our lives for the better, attracts others, gives us weight, and keeps us grounded in our purpose. Just as gravity is an invisible reality made visible by its effects, the same is true for holy gravity. The visible effects in our lives prove the existence of holy gravity. And just as gravity is not man-made, neither is holy gravity; it comes from God.

Think of gravity pulling an apple to the ground when it falls from a tree. The apple does not pull itself down, nor can it create new ways of getting to the ground without gravity. In the same way, we cannot ground ourselves. The moment sin entered the world, God knew we would be helpless and hopeless, lost in the vastness of our sin forever if He didn't intercede. But He did intercede. In love, He sent Jesus to make a way for us to live grounded in holy gravity through His life, death, and resurrection from the dead. Without Jesus, we would have no desire or ability to draw ourselves to God just like the apple cannot draw itself to the ground without gravity doing its work. But when we believe in Jesus Christ, trusting His death and resurrection as the means through which we can know God and commune with Him, we live in holy gravity and fulfill God's purpose for our lives.

Holy Gravity and the Fear of God

How is holy gravity related to the fear of God? There are innumerable small purposes that God will accomplish in His people when they trust in Him. In the quote opening this chapter, Oswald Chambers explains that the fulfillment of God's good purpose for our lives is in and through a relationship with Jesus Christ. The ultimate good purpose fulfilled through an intimate relationship with Jesus Christ is an understanding of the fear of God and an application of that fear. Solomon made this point at the end of the book of Ecclesiastes. He said, "The end of the matter; all has been heard. Fear God and keep his commandments, for this is the whole duty of man" (Ecclesiastes 12:13). The pinnacle of Solomon's wisdom is to fear God and keep His commandments. God created us to fear Him and keep His commandments.

If fearing God is so significant, so ultimate, why are we satisfied to know so little about this command? The command to fear God is clear throughout Scripture, yet we have settled for a surface-level understanding of what it means. The circumstances in my own life prompted me to probe into this command, asking the Lord to teach me more about what it means to fear Him. In studying to write this book, I was amazed by all I was missing in this seemingly simple albeit confusing command, most significantly its connection to our holiness. The more I learned, the more I grieved the unsurprising effects in my life, in the lives of those around me, and in the world, of our neglect of and apathy for God and fearing Him.

God's Word confirms over and over again that the fear of God is intimately connected with turning from sin or evil and obeying His commands. These are impossible tasks for sinful people to do on our own, and we're proving that every day. Within God's sovereign control, the world seems to be falling apart; even churches are dividing, falling away, or fitting the illustration, floating away from gravity. The absence of the fear of God will lead to sin, and sin always has a tragic trickle-down effect. But the contrast is also true: the presence of the fear of God leads to holiness through Jesus Christ. His life gives us joy and peace that will have the most beautiful ripple effect as others become beneficiaries of these graces from God too.

The Gravity of Holy Gravity

This book recognizes holy gravity as coming from Jesus Christ as His Spirit equips us to fear God. In addition, this book also communicates the weightiness and significance of this call to fear God. It is not an option for God's people; it is a command—it is our whole duty. Those who love God will fear Him, and those who fear Him will love Him, and they will be marked by His holiness. Just like gravity is not seen, but its effects are obvious, we do not see God, but His work in His people is obvious. That evidence is holiness in the fear of God. It is proof of the presence of God in our lives.

We cannot deny that we will not always demonstrate this holiness on this side of heaven because we still battle against our flesh in this evil world, even as believers in Jesus Christ. We will fail and fall short of this high call every day. We will float off when we yield to our temptations to sin. We must ask ourselves this: Do I care enough about God? Do I love and fear Him enough to turn back to Him with help from His Spirit when I sin against Him? He loved me enough to make that turning back even possible, and He will always receive me when I come with my sinful heart, asking Him to purify it. Will I trust that only through my relationship with Jesus Christ can God equip me to fulfill the good purposes, both singular and plural, in my life? As we live each day grounded in Him, we will testify to His faithfulness and live in the joyful, peaceful, and satisfying place of holy gravity.

I pray *Holy Gravity*, with Scripture as its foundation and authority, will exhort and equip us, as we are all in some way floating about. May we abide in Jesus Christ, who will always return His people to God's good and loving purposes as we grow in holiness through the fear of God for His glory, forever and ever. Amen.

PART I

Understanding the Fear of God

CHAPTER 1

The Mystery of Fearing God

"Call to me and I will answer you and will tell you great and hidden things that you have not known." Jeremiah 33:3

"Our only hope of knowing God truly is that He should be graciously pleased to reveal Himself to us, and the Christian teaching is that God has done that." Martyn Lloyd-Jones[2]

Finite minds cannot understand infinite truth. Knowing we are limited, however, does not excuse us from God's commands. The command to fear God is mysterious, clouded by all that we don't know about God and His ways, which are higher than ours (Isaiah 55:8-9). Naturally, we fall short when we make efforts to keep God's commands on our own. When we try to understand God, His Word, and His commands, we usually discover just how much we don't know. The critical question is this: What do we do when met with the vast unknown?

Three paths are available to us regarding our understanding of God and His commands. First is the path of ignorance. This is the wide and easy way of the world, but even most Christians would readily admit the Bible is full of truths too complicated for us. We may even avoid studying difficult topics and declare that the Bible tells us some things are too wonderful for us to understand (Job 42:3). At the same time we must also confess that the Bible also tells us that God reveals truth and mystery (Daniel 2:28, Amos 3:7, Matthew 13:11, and more). It is our choice to seek the truth or resign ourselves to ignorance. If we choose the latter, we cannot make progress.

---

[2] Lloyd-Jones, Martyn. 2012. *Great Doctrines of the Bible (Three Volumes in One): God the Father, God the Son; God the Holy Spirit; The Church and the Last Things*. Crossway.

The second path pursues knowledge as the ultimate end. Solomon warned that the acquisition of wisdom and knowledge is a striving after wind (Ecclesiastes 1:16-17). All the information available constantly cannot satiate those hungry for knowledge; they always want more. As a nerdy teacher type, I find myself buying pens all the time. They aren't the same kind; they are all different: felt tip, gel, colorful, plain, fat tip, thin tip. The problem with constantly buying pens of any kind is that I cannot use them all. I simply acquire them and do nothing but admire them. I use some, but far too many serve no purpose. Knowledge-seekers, striving after wind, similarly fall short of applying their knowledge and constantly seek to acquire more. Just like the path of ignorance, this path is futile to understanding eternal things.

Finally, we have a third path. It's not the way of ignorance nor the knowledge-seeker's way. It is a narrow path leading us to truth which reveals God's mysteries. It's a paradoxical path in which we understand that we cannot understand, but we should pursue understanding.

Admitting the Mystery

> "Job is comforted with riddles; but he is comforted. Herein is indeed a type, in a sense of a prophecy, of things speaking with authority. For when he who doubts can only say, 'I do not understand,' it is true that he who knows can only reply or repeat 'You do not understand.' And under that rebuke there is always a sudden hope in the heart; and the sense of something that would be worth understanding." G. K. Chesterton[3]

Our world today perfectly displays the tragic effects of remaining ignorant of God's mysteries. We can choose to remain ignorant or confess that our feeble minds are limited in our understanding of God, His Word, and His commands, but we desire to understand. The latter is not an empty confession that makes no effort to pursue understanding. It's an admission that we don't understand but we don't want to stay in our ignorance. In this acknowledgment, the mystery brings with it a sense of urgency and longing.

There's great wisdom in admitting we understand that we cannot understand. Our confession acknowledges that we don't have all the answers and marks the realization that we cannot acquire those answers on our own.

---

[3] Chesterton, G. K. 2021. *The Everlasting Man*. Canon Press.

But Christians are to grow in our knowledge and understanding of God and His Word, so we should pursue understanding. We cannot stop with simply confessing that we cannot understand and expect to grow in our knowledge of God. For Christians, with our admission of ignorance comes a conviction from the Holy Spirit that propels us to seek to grow in the grace and knowledge of our Lord and Savior Jesus Christ (2 Peter 3:18) and a craving for pure spiritual milk that will grow us in our salvation (1 Peter 2:2). There is necessary humility in our confession that the command to fear God is beyond our understanding. It puts us in a position to depend on God's wisdom to understand and obey it.

God's Word Reveals the Mystery

> "I became a minister according to the stewardship from God that was given to me for you, to make the word of God fully known, the mystery hidden for ages and generations but now revealed to his saints." Colossians 1:25-26

Many seek wisdom and understanding about God, apart from God. When they pursue knowledge, what they come to know is not God or God's ways because you cannot understand God, His commands, or His ways apart from Him. Scripture tells us, "The sum of your word is truth, and every one of your righteous rules endures forever" (Psalm 119:160). God gave us His Word so that by it, we can know the truth and therefore, we can know Him. When our understanding is apart from God's Word, our understanding is faulty. When founded on God's Word, our understanding will have a transforming effect on our lives.

The world denies the truth of God's Word yet claims to understand eternal things like love and salvation and God Himself, among other things. Even Christians sometimes neglect God's Word because we become comfortable with our religious lives and our basic understanding of truths God wants us to know on a far deeper level. Like a child who tires of her mother's constant instructions, we can tire of listening to God's commands and tune Him out when we think we already "got it." But we must diligently pursue understanding truth, no matter how mysterious or seemingly understood, because truth is foundational to fearing God.

When we come to understand the truth through the Word, the evidence of our understanding will be a God-given desire to know the Word and to make Him fully known. Paul became a minister of the gospel "to make the word of God fully known, the mystery hidden for ages and generations but now revealed to His saints" (Colossians 1:25-26). The Word is available to us, and the mystery doesn't have to be mysterious to His saints. He has already been revealed.

The Evidence of Understanding

> "To them God chose to make known how great among the Gentiles are the riches of the glory of this mystery, which is Christ in you, the hope of glory." Colossians 1:27

It is to the saints that "God chose to make known how great among the Gentiles are the riches of the glory of this mystery, which is Christ in you, the hope of glory" (Colossians 1:27). So, are we talking about the mystery of God's command to fear Him or the mystery of the gospel revealed to the saints through Christ in us, the hope of glory? I submit they are one and the same. Our power to fear God comes from Christ in us. The fear of God will manifest itself externally, though it begins with Christ within. Those who fear God are those to whom the mystery has been revealed. The believer will aim to know this mystery better and, with equal gravity and conviction, make this mystery known to other people.

Understanding the Mystery That Leads to Maturity

> "Him we proclaim, warning everyone and teaching everyone with all wisdom, that we may present everyone mature in Christ." Colossians 1:28

The world is lost. Even churches are full of lost and discouraged people who live so much of life in a seemingly contradictory state between what they say and how they live. Some long to be grounded in Christ yet their understanding of what that means remains clouded in mystery. Paul recognized the urgency of making this mystery known. He emphasized the importance of proclaiming Christ to all, knowing the end goal of our proclamation is maturity in Christ, proof that the mystery is no longer a mystery but revealed.

Proclaiming Christ necessarily includes warning and teaching everyone with all wisdom. The reason for proclaiming Christ, through warning and teaching with His wisdom, is "that we may present everyone mature in Christ." The world tells us we should love as they imagine love, but we are to love as God calls us to love. Loving others will sometimes mean that we warn them. We warn them of the eternal consequences of living apart from Christ now and forever. Loving others will also mean that we teach them. Paul says we teach everyone, not just certain people. We cannot assess with our finite, human wisdom who will hear the gospel and receive it, therefore we cannot exclude anyone from hearing the gospel. We must yield to God and His complete wisdom as we teach everyone. As we teach, we do so with all wisdom. This call to teach with all wisdom reminds us that the content of what we teach and the understanding by which we have come to know it is not our own. It comes from the source of all wisdom.

"Warning everyone and teaching everyone" is a significant statement. The command is not just to warn the lost and teach the Christian but also to warn the Christian and teach the lost. This command again speaks to the significance and weightiness of our role as Christ-followers in the Church and in the world: to lead those around us to maturity in Christ. God's Word often speaks about maturity, specifically maturity in Christ. The term "mature" in this verse can also translate to "complete" (NASB) or "perfect" (NIV, NKJV). Consider these translations and the number of exhortations in Scripture concerning our growth—to grow up and not remain infants, to grow in the grace and knowledge of our Lord Jesus Christ, to consecrate ourselves before God, and to be holy as He is holy. We find maturity in Christ is the goal of our Christian faith—our sanctification and holiness for God's glory. It should be our goal to mature in Christ and present everyone around us as mature in Christ.

We are to mature past infancy once we are regenerated and receive the Holy Spirit. When we pray for salvation through Jesus Christ, it is then that we begin to work out our own salvation with fear and trembling (Philippians 2:12). By the grace of God, we will grow and mature in holiness and help those around us grow and mature in holiness. We mature in holiness through the fear of God (2 Corinthians 7:1). The more we grow in Christ, the more we fear God; and the more we fear God, the more we grow in Christ.

The Messengers and Hearers of This Mystery

> "For this I toil, struggling with all his energy that he powerfully works within me." Colossians 1:29

Paul finishes explaining his ministry to the church by reiterating that making the mystery of Christ in us known is the reason for his life's work. He also identifies how maturation, or sanctification, happens: It doesn't happen by trying to check off a Bible to-do list. It doesn't happen by pleasing man, though we often work in vain toward that goal. We grow and mature through the work of the Holy Spirit in our lives. It is "His" energy that "He" powerfully works in us; this explains how the Spirit works through the messengers. The messengers toil to mature the Church with the Spirit's energy, but what about the hearers? How do those who hear mature? We can go back to the first part of Paul's mission: We seek to know the Word of God. This means we study Scripture to know it, and in doing so, we know better the Word Himself: Jesus Christ. Christ works within us to mature us, and the Church around us will also mature in the process.

The messengers and hearers become the same people. The messengers are at first hearers, and the hearers become messengers. As time goes on, together they proclaim Christ to all as more hearers also become messengers. It's important to note that the messengers never cease to be hearers; the all-inclusive "everyone" includes the messengers. The messengers also have ears to hear both warning and teaching from the source of all wisdom. We must always seek to know God better through His Word because maturity, or sanctification, is a continuous process that moves us toward glorification, "the hope of glory." We don't graduate from being hearers once we become messengers. As messengers, we proclaim Christ to all; as those with ears to hear, we receive the truth of His proclamations that the work of the Spirit may sanctify us all and reveal the mystery of Christ in us.

"Christ in us" is the means through which we fear God. Understanding this mystery is a life-long endeavor that leads us from glory to glory, but it begins and continues with our submission to the God of glory for the glory of God.

CHAPTER 2

The Significance of Holiness

"Worship the LORD in the splendor of holiness; tremble before him, all the earth." Psalm 96:9

"No attribute of God is more dreadful to sinners than His holiness." Matthew Henry[4]

God's holiness is at the heart of our fear of Him. We are to fear God because He is worthy to be feared in all His glory. But that is the problem—we don't fear Him rightly because we don't see Him completely in all His glory. We focus only on some of His attributes while overlooking others. Because we are finite beings, what we see is often clouded by our imperfect and incomplete perceptions of who He really is.

We have lost sight of much of God's character which has dramatically and devastatingly impacted our world, the Church, and our lives at the most personal and intimate levels. Some of His attributes have been intentionally ignored or ignorantly misunderstood. By losing sight of God's holiness, deliberately or innocently, we may be doing the most damage to our souls. God's holiness is not merely one of His attributes but the compilation of all of His attributes: wisdom, love, mercy, justice, sovereignty, and more in their purest and perfect form. A perfect form is the only form God's attributes can take. He is either perfectly sovereign (in control of all things) or not sovereign at all. To add "perfectly" is redundant. And that is the case for each of His attributes. If God is not pure and perfect wisdom, then He is not wisdom.

---

[4] Henry, Matthew. 2008. *Matthew Henry's Commentary on the Whole Bible: Complete and Unabridged.* Hendrickson Publishers.

If He is not pure and perfect love, He is not love. The whole of who God is in His purity and totality of goodness is His holiness. Holiness defines His very nature, and His holiness is at the heart of our proper fear of Him. As we have lost sight of His holiness and complete and perfect nature, we have consequently lost our fear of Him.

Holiness and Fear

> "Therefore, having these promises, beloved, let us cleanse ourselves from all filthiness of the flesh and spirit, perfecting holiness in the fear of God." 2 Corinthians 7:1 (NASB)

Scripture commands us to fear God, but without connecting the dots between fearing God and our holiness, we miss a significant aspect of what it truly means to fear Him. When Scripture repeatedly commands us to fear the Lord, we usually ask what it means. While this is undoubtedly an important question, the more I studied this topic the more I realized a more meaningful question for us to consider might be, "What does it look like?" This book explores how fearing God looks like holy living. Holy lives are God-fearing lives.

We often place ourselves in one of two camps: the "I got this" camp or the "no chance" camp. In the "I got this" camp, we feel confident about our progress and ability to live a holy life. The "no chance" camp, on the other hand, denies any possibility that we would be called by God to live a holy and set apart life. The chapters in this book, however, do not make such a clear distinction. We fall into both camps all the time. Pride puts us in the first, and unbelief puts us in the second. Christians and unbelievers can both encounter the temptation to live in either camp. The Spirit of God wants to put us on a whole different plane.

The chapters in this book elevate us to that new and different plane—a plane that believes the truth of God's Word, which tells that we are unholy because of our sin, yet, by the blood of Jesus Christ, His holiness becomes ours. Scripture draws out four marks in the life of the one who fears God and, in doing so, lives a holy life: wisdom, love, obedience, and suffering. Like any subject in Scripture, we could cover so much and still not exhaust God's instructions. But His instructions are clear: it is His holiness—His character—that He calls us to demonstrate when we fear God. His wisdom and love prove His holiness, and we show them through our obedience to His Word and Spirit, no matter the circumstances of our lives.

Christ's Holiness and His People

> "Holiness is not the way to Christ; Christ is the way to holiness."
> Adrian Rogers[5]

One of the most destructive lies we believe today is rooted in a half-truth. Satan's best strategies to destroy the Church, beginning in the Garden of Eden, come through half-truths. The lie/half-truth is this: Christ's holiness is His alone, and we have no part in it. It's true that "no one is righteous" (Ecclesiastes 7:20). "We all have sinned and fall short of the glory of God" (Romans 3:23). "No one does good" (Psalm 14:1-3, 53:1). Each of these verses confirms we are not holy by nature. The Bible tells us only One is holy: "The Lord, our Redeemer, is the Holy One of Israel" (Isaiah 41:14). Not only is the Lord the Holy One, but Scripture also tells us "His glory He will not give to another" (Isaiah 48:11). This last verse seems to only confirm the idea that Christ's holiness is His alone, and we have no part in it. But the lie that has seeped into our understanding of the truth is that we can look to Christ's holiness alone and not live holy lives ourselves. This thinking suggests we should always look to Christ's holiness but not feel obligated to pursue it because we can't achieve or attain it. But God commands us to be holy as He is holy (Leviticus 19:2) and to consecrate, or purify, ourselves (Joshua 3:5, Isaiah 1:16, James 4:8). Consider also that all the commands in Scripture call us to obedience so that we may live holy lives. We are to look to Christ in all His glory *and* pursue holiness in Him as long as we are on this earth. The two are inseparable. As long as Christ is our first pursuit, holiness will naturally follow.

I was in a small discussion group studying Philippians 4. At one point we focused on verses 8 and 9: "Finally, brothers, whatever is true, whatever is honorable, whatever is just, whatever is pure, whatever is lovely, whatever is commendable, if there is any excellence, if there is anything worthy of praise, think about these things. What you have learned and received and heard and seen in me—practice these things, and the God of peace will be

---

[5] Rogers, Adrian. "Christ Is the Way to Holiness." Love Worth Finding. June 1, 2018. Retrieved from https://www.lwf.org/daily-devotions/christ-is-the-way-to-holiness.

with you." I was struck by verse 9 in a way I had never been before. Paul was speaking to the Philippians, telling them to practice what they had learned and received and what they had heard and seen in him. What a bold statement. Giving similar instructions to the Church throughout his ministry, he told the Corinthian church to imitate him as he imitated Christ (1 Corinthians 4:16, 1 Corinthians 11:1). I commented to the group how convicting that was that Paul encouraged and exhorted them to live as he lived and as he taught. He walked the walk and called them to follow. What walk could he call them to other than a walk worthy of the calling to which we have been called—holiness by the Spirit in us? It made me ask myself, "Could I tell others to do the same about my life?" Similarly, a Jewish rabbi's goal for his students was to multiply what they learned from him and apply it by "following him" in life. And isn't that precisely what Jesus told his disciples when He said to them, "Follow Me"? It is a command to imitate His life, not merely to listen to His words and tell others the same words, but to live His life, go in the direction He wants us to go, and do what He says.

One of the ladies responded to my comment saying we should look to Christ. There is the obvious danger of focusing on our own efforts toward righteousness, which are always in vain, and the temptation toward pride when others admire us and our lives. I think she was speaking from the valid concern that people shouldn't be focused on us; they should focus on Jesus. But God's people are the means through which the world can see Jesus Christ. I think Satan has tried to establish in our churches the idea that Christ is holy but doesn't mean to manifest His holiness in us today. And yet that is the very purpose of our lives—to fear God and keep His commandments, to love the Lord with all our heart, soul, and mind, to love our neighbor as ourselves, to do what He says, to do everything for the glory of God, to let our light shine before men that God may receive the glory. It is not our holiness but the holiness of Christ, who is the image of the invisible God. Christ in us is what we are calling the world to see. Not ourselves, but Christ in us. He is our light that shines in the darkness. God did not mean for Christ's life to only secure our salvation, but for His life to be lived in us before the world so that others might know the glory of God shown in the face of Jesus Christ, who lives in those who believe in Him. Christ's holiness is the Christian's holiness. And we are to become the righteousness of Christ, not primarily for our benefits though they are innumerable. Living in Christ benefits those around us who see His holiness and can receive it through faith. To say God's holiness is at the heart of our proper fear of Him means that His holiness fills our hearts, and that same holiness manifests for the world to see.

God's Holiness and Our Unholiness

> "We shall never be clothed with the righteousness of Christ except we first know assuredly that we have no righteousness of our own." John Calvin[6]

While God's holiness is central to our fear of Him, that fear directly correlates to our holiness. The more we see and know His holiness, the more we fear Him; and the more we fear Him, the more we grow in holiness. Recognizing His holiness is the first step in confessing our unholiness. We see the standard we cannot meet. The standard our holy God demands. We cannot become holy without acknowledging His holiness and confessing our unholiness. It is through the affirmation of His holiness and the grief over our unholiness that His righteousness becomes ours, only made possible by the blood of Jesus shed on the cross. God revealing Himself to us is so significant because He is making a way for us to know Him and commune with Him as we live our lives in holy fear.

---

[6] Calvin, John. 2012. *Commentary on Romans*. Ravenio Books.

---— CHAPTER 3 ———

Knowing God

*"And this is eternal life, that they know you, the only true God,
and Jesus Christ, whom you have sent." John 17:3*

*"The world becomes a strange, mad, and painful place and life in it is a disappointing
and unpleasant business for those who do not know about God. Disregard the
study of God, and you sentence yourself to stumble and blunder through life
blindfolded as it were, with no sense of direction and no understanding of what
surrounds you. This way you can waste your life and lose your soul." J. I. Packer*[7]

We can only fear God if we know Him. The more we know God, the more we can fear Him, and the more complete our fear of Him will be. But knowing God is not simply being aware of God or faithfully reading about Him. Most Americans say they believe in God. That statistic includes believing in the God of the Bible but also the belief in a general higher being/power. Even among those who say they believe in the God of the Bible, there is considerable variation in their understanding of God. Whether men or women, Protestant or Jewish, Democrat or Republican, their views of God could all be different. We live in a time that places great value on our external descriptives to the point where they define us more than the thoughts and attitudes of our hearts. The friends with whom we associate, the leaders to whom we listen, teachings under which we sit can shape our view of God, but those external factors don't change who God is, only our perceptions of who He is. Do those who believe in the God of the Bible know the same God? If so, why is there so much subjectivity in their view of Him?

---

[7] Packer, J. I. 1973. *Knowing God.* InterVarsity.

An Objective God

> "Jesus Christ is the same yesterday and today and forever."
> Hebrews 13:8

God is objective and unchanging. His Word that tells us about Him is objective and unchanging. His character is constant. Who He is in the Old Testament is the same as who He is in the New Testament; He is that same God today who doesn't change. So why do so many see Him differently? This question leads to an essential question about our belief in God. Why do so many professing Christians see God differently? Among denominations, we could easily find pastors, priests, and ministers who view God differently by how they interpret Scripture.

We often view God and His Word through our personal experiences or ideas, which is like wearing distorted glasses. They might be rose-colored or like wacky mirrors you find in the mirror mazes at a fair. Those glasses don't change what we see, only how we see it. God intended every word in Scripture, which ultimately reveals Himself, to be understood with crystal clear lenses, those lenses being the wisdom of the Spirit. We bring to the text of His Word a thousand different distorted lenses, but we must ask God alone to help us take off those lenses and, with His help, see Him and His Word in the right way He intended.

We can have a right view of God and a right view of truth or a wrong view of God and a wrong view of truth. What does this mean for us seeking to know God? It means there is a right answer. It's not multiple choice or "all of the above" but one right, objective, and unchanging truth that leads us to the One right, objective, and unchanging God. How can we ensure we know the right and true God and not a fabrication of our minds? I think we can know in two ways:

1. The Holy Spirit is one with God. He is God and dwells in all who believe in Jesus Christ. The Holy Spirit cannot disagree with Himself; therefore, when we speak of who God is, based on His Word, the Spirit of God in His people will agree on all foundational things of the faith. There will be unity and peace in their knowledge of God because of the truth.
2. Within the Church there will be minor areas of disagreement, but how individuals respond to these disagreements will also speak of our knowledge of the One True God. John 13:35 says, "By this all men will

know that you are my disciples, if you have love for one another." Knowing the One True God means the Holy Spirit empowers us to live and love like Jesus Christ Himself, even during times of disagreement. This testimony will be so clear that *all* people will know we belong to God.

Proof That We Know God

Many in the world today say they know God, but unless they know the One True God we find in Scripture and come to know Him through faith in Jesus Christ by the work of the Holy Spirit, they only know an idol. Even in churches, we have sometimes misunderstood what it means to know God and how that true knowledge will look in our lives. This discrepancy should compel us to seek to know the truth. When the God of all wisdom warns us and teaches us through His Word, we mature before the world and prove to those around us we know God. The more we know God, the more we mature in Christ or grow in holiness. Our maturity is a product of an ever-increasing fear of God.

We understand who God is through our inseparable relationship with Jesus Christ, who is the wisdom through whom we are warned and taught. I can know God because I know the truth. I can know the truth because I know Christ. If someone told me about the character of a celebrity, I couldn't accurately determine what was true and what was false without knowing her myself. My relationship with her would help me discern what was true or false. Similarly, through my personal relationship with Jesus Christ, I can know the truth about who God is. If I know Jesus Christ, I know God. And knowing God is the first step to fearing Him rightly.

The Right Kind of Experience

> "But you will receive power when the Holy Spirit has come upon you, and you will be my witnesses in Jerusalem and in all Judea and Samaria, and to the end of the earth." Acts 1:8

While our life experiences can mislead us, personally experiencing God will grow our faith and equip us to lead others in the right direction (toward Him) so they too can experience Him personally and fear Him rightly. We cannot manufacture a right and holy fear of God. It comes through that intimate and personal experience with Jesus Christ and His work in our lives. Think of when you entered a new stage in life—beginning college, starting a new job, getting married, becoming a parent. Many likely advised on how to thrive in that stage, whether it was requested or not. You may have done research to prepare. The counsel and research were likely helpful, but they didn't compare to all you learned through experience. Second-hand information is much different than first-hand eyewitness experience.

I remember the major contrast between my idea of motherhood and the reality of motherhood. Until I lost sleep, missed meals, gave up many of my past responsibilities, doubled my laundry, and shifted some of my focus off myself to my dependent baby, I couldn't have articulated the challenges of motherhood. Maybe intellectually, I could, but not experientially. Until I heard her first cry, saw her first smile, struggled through potty training, and walked her into her kindergarten classroom, I couldn't have articulated, with meaningful understanding, some of motherhood's great joys and challenges. I needed to experience them for myself.

First-hand experience changes your intellectual knowledge. Hearing about a car accident is different than seeing it happen with your own eyes, which is also different than being in a car accident. That personal connection to the experience impacts you. When you are an eyewitness to the stress of unexpected trials in your marriage, the inexpressible joy of holding your child for the first time, or the debilitating pain of losing someone you love, it changes you. Though comments like, "It's so wonderful!" or "It's so hard," may affect your perception, the experience has the greatest impact on your life, and that experience changes you.

Could this be what Jesus meant when He told his disciples and all those who would trust Him as LORD that "You will receive power when the Holy Spirit has come upon you, and you will be my witnesses in Jerusalem and in all Judea and Samaria and to the end of the earth" (Acts 1:8)? We receive the power of God through the Holy Spirit when we have a relationship with Christ. That Spirit powerfully works in us, and we are eyewitnesses to the Spirit's work as we see Him change our lives and the lives of those around us as we proclaim Christ. Unless the Holy Spirit has made us new creations, we cannot witness God's saving work in our lives.

Until we experience God through our relationship with Jesus Christ in the Person of the Holy Spirit, we cannot truly know God the way He intends. We must seek the truth, receive the Spirit, and be eyewitnesses to His powerful work as He changes us from the inside out. If there's no change, there's no fear.

CHAPTER 4

Two Fears

"For you did not receive the spirit of slavery to fall back into fear, but you have received the Spirit of adoption as sons, by whom we cry, "Abba! Father!" Romans 8:15

"We must fear God out of love, not love Him out of fear." St. Francis de Sales[8]

While we usually think of fear as bad, the biblical worldview necessarily includes good fear: the fear of the LORD. Martin Luther established two classifications for fear which help us understand the fear of God. He called these fears servile fear and filial fear. Servile fear is rooted in negative emotions. Luther described this fear as a prisoner's fear of his tormentor or a slave's of his evil master. The prisoner's ultimate fear is punishment. On a superficial level, this is the fear the world thinks Christians have for God. They think Christians live and act a certain way only to avoid punishment from God.

In contrast, filial fear, from the Latin word for family, is the good fear a child has toward her father. She fears offending or disappointing him because she deeply loves and respects him. This good fear drives her to act in a way that honors him. Christians can understand this fear based on their knowledge of God who loves us and gave up His only Son for us. We revere Him and want to please Him because we love Him, not because we fear punishment.[9]

---

[8] Camus, Jean P. 2016. *The Spirit of St. Francis De Sales*. CreateSpace Independent Publishing.

[9] Sproul, R. C. "Throughout the Bible We Are Told to Fear God. What Does That Mean?" *Ligonier Ministries,* http://www.ligonier.org/learn/qas/throughout-bible-we-are-told-fear-god-what-does-me. Accessed autumn 2019.

Comparing Servile and Filial Fear

When comparing these two types of fear, we better distinguish filial fear as the right and holy fear before God. It is born out of reverence for His glory, trust in His sovereignty, awe of His majesty, humility because of His mercy, gratitude because of His grace, and submission because of His love. It is a fear that focuses on God, who He is, and what He has done. It is all about Him, and that is a fundamental distinction between these two fears. While both may acknowledge a master, the object of value in each fear is very different.

Filial fear recognizes God as most worthy and valuable. It is not a fear focused on ourselves, concerned for the consequences we might face for our actions or the circumstances in which we find ourselves. When we fear God, we will not focus on ourselves, our situation, or circumstances because our focus is on Him and His work in and through us. He is our object of greatest value, and His glory is our greatest desire. The one who fears God has a love for Him that supersedes any other. It is an all-consuming fear or love that desires to please Him and not grieve Him. Scripture commands us to demonstrate this fear of God in our lives.

Conversely, servile fear is not most concerned about God. The object of greatest value is ourselves. Servile fear focuses more on how circumstances will negatively affect us. Our behavior is not driven by love and reverence for God but by avoiding bad things. The unbeliever's concern is for herself, while the Christian's concern, when Spirit-filled, will be for God and His praise and glory. We might think, then, that unbelievers have servile fear of God and believers have filial fear of God and wrap up the discussion. But we can't draw a broad conclusion that says unbelievers have servile fear of God and believers have filial fear of God because servile fear of God still acknowledges Him and His authority to execute justice.

Servile Fear as a Stepping-Stone

Luther's classifications seem contradictory. We may conclude that servile fear has no place in Christians' lives because Christians are not prisoners of a tormenting God. However, if we only ever have servile fear and behave out of fear of punishment, then we are driven by the punishment, not God's love.

But if we completely write off servile fear, we miss Luther's point. It's not an "either," "or" for the Christian, but a "both," "and."

God is not an evil master who delights in punishment (Ezekiel 33:11). He never does His children wrong but acts for their good. Those in Christ have no reason to fear that God will forsake or condemn them because there is no condemnation for those in Christ Jesus (Romans 8:1). But God is terrifying in His holiness and justice, and Luther offers a critical point of clarification regarding these fears:

> For how fear of punishment and the fear of God differ is more easily said in syllables and letters than known in reality and affection. All believers fear punishment and hell. God will be with those who are His so that they fear God and punishment simultaneously. There can be no fear of God in this life without fear of punishment, as there can also be no spirit without flesh, though the fear of punishment is useless without the fear of God.[10]

Luther makes many significant points here:

1. Fear of punishment and fear of God can co-exist.
2. Believers are not suddenly free from fear of punishment and hell once they believe and trust Christ as Savior. (It's important to note believers will not receive the punishment, but as he mentions later in the quote, they will still struggle with the fear of punishment in their flesh.)
3. God will be with His children. He is not apathetic to their needs.
4. Fear of God cannot come without fear of punishment.
5. The fear of punishment, servile fear alone, profits nothing without the fear of God. Fear of punishment doesn't save us.

Luther addresses the fact that believers will fear punishment while also fearing God. While there's reverence, awe, and humility before Him, there is terror at the idea of spending eternity apart from Him. Experiencing His goodness and grace, Christians are made aware of their sin by the conviction of the Holy Spirit. They are increasingly aware of the wages they deserve (death)

---

[10] Peters, Albrecht. 2009. *Commentary on Luther's Catechisms: Ten Commandments.* Concordia Publishing.

apart from Christ. Through their study of Scripture, they know the reality of life without Him, though they can't imagine just how awful it would be. In all this, God has opened their eyes to Him as more than a disengaged God.

The Gospel and Servile Fear

The world sees God in many incorrect ways, with many distorted lenses. Besides the lens of a mean tormenter, another lens sees Him as an apathetic Being who cares very little about His creation, what we do, or how we live. Christians may face the temptation to put on these lenses and, in doing so, travel down a dangerous path. The idea that God is malicious to His people or doesn't care about His creation, what we do, or how we live is a lie. Satan wants us to believe these lies more than anything. He wants us to be so distracted with our wrong ideas about God that we end up with no fear of Him at all. Why would keeping us from either type of fear be so valuable to Satan? Because even servile fear has great value in leading a believer to filial fear.

Servile fear is the initial fear every Christ-follower has because our response to the gospel begins with an awareness that we are sinners who deserve punishment and death. We should rightfully be separated from God apart from Jesus Christ because we can never be holy as He is holy apart from the work of Christ in us. And while servile fear doesn't save us, it should propel us to see our sins in light of a holy and glorious God.

Luther's initial definitions make it sound like servile fear—fear of punishment—is not the right fear to have before God. While ultimately true, God uses servile fear to lead us to filial fear, fear of offending Him because we love Him. When we hear the gospel and the Holy Spirit stirs our hearts, we receive eyes to see and hearts that fear Him first in a servile way. Each of us has sinned and, without Christ, deserves death. Through the Holy Spirit's revelation, Christians are aware of their sins and the holiness of God. While complete comprehension of these truths is impossible on this side of heaven, the ever-deepening knowledge of both their sin and God's holiness drives them to fear God more. Servile fear is present, not because God is an evil master seeking punishment, but because we are in a battle between the flesh and the Spirit.

The turning of a Christian's heart away from sin and toward God is not motivated by the fear of punishment but by the fear of God Himself. In the case of filial fear, we are grieved over our sin because we have not pleased Him, yet we still run to Him in repentance, knowing that remaining close to Him is the only way to rid ourselves of the sin that so easily entangles us. We look to Him expectantly for wisdom to help us live in a way that pleases Him. And He is faithful to guide, but even more, empower us to trust Him completely because we know He loves us. Luther's terms help those in Christ see God as a loving Father who, though we sin, stands ready to forgive us. Knowing God is holy and just and will not let a sinner's deeds go unpunished drives the Christian to bow before God with a filial fear that comes from the Spirit.

You cannot separate God's attributes, such as His perfection, holiness, justice, and goodness, from His love, mercy, and grace. He is One, and His attributes co-exist in Him together at the same time, every time. Fear of His punishment will be present in His people, but it will not overcome us because His Spirit will give us His peace and righteousness, freeing us from the punishment for which Jesus Christ atoned. By the power and wisdom of the Holy Spirit, the Christian understands who God is and, therefore, can know what to fear. The unbeliever doesn't know God, so they don't know what to fear. They live apart from God, though not apart from His sovereign command of their lives.

CHAPTER 5

The Fearless

"They have not humbled themselves even to this day, nor have they feared, nor walked in my law and my statutes that I set before you and before your fathers." Jeremiah 44:10

"When men no longer fear God, they transgress His laws without hesitation. The fear of consequences is no deterrent when the fear of God is gone." A. W. Tozer[11]

One interesting and necessary observation we should make as we look at Luther's two classifications is that, in most cases, neither servile fear nor filial fear is present in the life of one who rejects God. We cannot assume one is the way Christians fear God and the other is how unbelievers fear God. The real tragedy is having no fear of God at all. Many today find no fault within themselves, removing any reason in their minds to fear God. We can certainly agree with David when he said, "there is no fear of God before [their] eyes" (Psalm 36:1).

No Servile Fear

Apathy regarding punishment suffocates servile fear. Our culture has helped desensitize our consciences, so we believe very few of our behaviors deserve punishment. If we do face penalties or consequences, we often claim to be mistreated because we are acting according to what we think is right. We tend to justify our behavior in our minds. There is an authoritarian and

---

[11] Tozer, A. W. 1965. *The Knowledge of the Holy.* Fig.

subjective mindset in which the one who rejects God says, "I rule my own life, and if I think it's right and good, then it is." There is apathy toward God, His holiness, and His sovereignty. There is certainly no fear of punishment, or many would try to avoid it if they knew it was imminent.

No Filial Fear

Filial fear is also lacking in many cultures around the world. The fear of offending someone is rare when we are usually more focused on ourselves and doing what *we* think is right instead of doing what *is* right. Consider how the following would need to be true for filial fear to exist:

- Loving someone more than ourselves.
- Caring enough about another person's thoughts and feelings to avoid offending them.
- Consideration and appreciation for an objective truth (what is right).
- Willingness to let go of our preferences (not convictions) if they contradict those of the ones we love.

In a culture that promotes love of self above all, we consequently find it difficult to care about what others think, whether we offend them or not. If we cannot even love others enough to care about offending them, how can we possibly love God and live in a way that we might not offend Him but bring Him glory?

A Punishment Deserved

> "The nature of Christ's salvation is woefully misrepresented by the present-day evangelist. He announces a Savior from hell rather than a Savior from sin. And that is why so many are fatally deceived, for there are multitudes who wish to escape the Lake of Fire who have no desire to be delivered from their carnality and worldliness." A. W. Pink[12]

God is clear in His Word that many people call Him Lord who will ultimately be turned away, condemned forever because they never knew Christ

---

[12] Pink, A. W. 2001. *Studies in the Scriptures, Volume 9 of 17.* Sovereign Grace Publishers.

(Matthew 7:21-23). Why? I argue they never regarded God as one to punish them. There is tremendous value in servile fear for the believer because it is the first step toward salvation. We are sinners, separated from God by our sins. We deserve punishment for our sins because God's Law demands perfection. None of us can measure up to perfection, so whether we miss the mark by a short distance or long distance, we still miss the mark and deserve death (James 2:10). Those who think they are safe from God's punishment yet continue to live in sin and unrepentance have neither fear for God.

The ones who will be eternally separated from God are the ones who do not fear Him. All those who love God fear Him, and our fear of Him grows the more we know Him. Therefore, knowing God is an essential foundation for fearing Him. If we know nothing of God, how can we fear Him? The foolish don't understand this, nor do they care to gain understanding. Most today would rather live to please themselves and busy themselves with selfish pleasures with no interest in knowing God. If someone remains apathetic toward eternal things, they will be consumed by the temporal until it is too late to know God and fear Him.

One of Satan's most effective strategies is to keep people from diligently seeking God. The less they seek Him, the less they know Him, and the less they fear Him. When Christians proclaim Jesus Christ as the only hope of salvation, unbelievers look on carelessly because they don't even know what the day of judgment holds for those who reject Him. They don't consider themselves deserving of punishment because they don't see how they have sinned against God. The gospel is meaningless to them, so they do not fear.

The Fearless in Church

Fearing God is necessary for the Church to understand today because many people fill our church buildings worldwide, ignoring a servile fear of God. They have no fear of punishment because they only see God in part, focusing on His grace and forbearance. They have a clouded view of His justice, holiness, and omniscience. Many will die and stand before Christ in judgment, and He will not simply take them at their word when they say, "Yes, Lord, I believed in you. I told all my friends I did. I went to church. I led Bible studies. I served the poor. I did a good job." If they never experienced servile fear that led to filial fear for God which resulted in submission to Jesus Christ as Lord of their lives, the fear of the Lord was not in them. Instead, it was love for themselves; as a result, what drove them to "good works" was not the Holy Spirit but their flesh.

The God-Fearing Church

For our fear of God to be true and complete, we must have a full picture of His glory. That picture won't come until we see Jesus face to face, but we take steps closer to that fullness of glory every day. It comes with an increasing awareness of the truth of who God is and who we are—a lifelong endeavor. The greatness of God's glory is terrifying to the sinful heart but by God's grace, all who love Him do not fear Him with servile fear alone. Christ came to help move us from servile fear to filial fear. The necessary mark in this movement from servile fear to filial fear is a heart that wants to love, honor, and revere God.

There is a remnant whom God chose before the foundation of the world, who will hear the call to hope in Jesus Christ for salvation from sin and eternal life with God forever. The Holy Spirit will open their eyes to see the glory of God and their sin simultaneously. They will see the punishment they deserve if they don't turn from their sin to God. This beginning fear leads Christians to grow in love and reverence for the One who took the punishment of sin upon Himself. The Spirit works in their hearts to move them from a servile fear to a filial fear as their lives glorify Him more and more with every passing day. Fear must be present.

CHAPTER 6

The Right Fear Among Wrong Fears

"I sought the LORD, and he answered me and delivered me from all my fears." Psalm 34:4

"The fear of God is the death of every other fear; like a mighty lion, it chases all other fears before it." Charles Spurgeon[13]

What about all the "fear nots?" The Bible tells us that Christians are not to fear. We have probably heard sermons on not fearing far more than sermons on the command to fear God. The Christian is to be fearless, which seems to contradict the previous chapter. "Do not be afraid...," "fear not...," "you have not received a spirit of fear...." There are 365 commands to "fear not." It is the most common command in Scripture, which is why so much more has been written on the "fear nots" than the "fears." We could agree that the "fear nots" pertain to the wrong fears. But what type of fear, or fears, is God prohibiting? Can they all be grouped as wrong fears under one category? Is there an easier way to understand the proper fear we are to have before God without getting into all the details of servile and filial fear?

The Christian should pursue filial fear, but the believer cannot deny that the Bible is filled with many commands to fear not. Servile and filial fears are specific to our attitude towards God, but are not the only fears we face. God gives us many examples in His Word of fearful people filled with the kind of fear He didn't want in their lives. Think of when the spies went into the promised land. God told them not to fear (Numbers 14:9). They were afraid

---

[13] Spurgeon, Charles. "Self-Humbling." Sermon at Metropolitan Tabernacle Pulpit, May 5, 1867.

of the people in the land, afraid of the unknown, afraid for their lives. King David cried out to God in many psalms confessing his fears (Psalm 6:2-4; Psalm 34:4; Psalm 55:16, 22; Psalm 56:3-4). Jesus questioned the disciples when they were afraid on the boat in the storm (Mark 4:35-41), and the early church was commanded not to fear persecution (1 Peter 3:14), to name a few.

Found at the root of every "fear not" or "fear" command is either self-focused fear or God-focused fear. "Fear nots" relate to our posture toward things other than God; the "fears" relate to our proper posture toward God. Even Luther's two classifications for fear stem from one or the other. Servile fear focuses on the self, whereas filial fear focuses on God. Understanding the difference between self-focused and God-focused fear can help us distinguish wrong from right as we read and study God's Word.

The Terror of Self-Focused Fear

> "I sought the Lord, and he answered me and delivered me from all my fears." Psalm 34:4

Recognizing self-focused fears and God-focused fear can help us distinguish just about every verse that references fear in the Bible. Consider Psalm 34:4. If we are seeking the Lord, this verse tells us He delivers us from all our fears. Because God delivers us from sin to Himself, not the other way around, we can conclude that these are sinful, self-focused fears, not pleasing God-focused fear. The Hebrew word for fears here translates to "terror." It is a comfort to know that God can free us from our terrors, all the thoughts and situations that make us so afraid. God doesn't want us to live life terrified, and His answer to our terror is Himself.

When we seek the Lord, He answers us and delivers us from all the fears that keep us from fearing Him. When we seek Christ, by His power alone, He delivers us from self-focused fears and fills us with God-focused fear. Verses 9 and 10 later in Psalm 34 confirm this when David says, "Oh, fear the Lord, you his saints, for those who fear him have no lack! The young lions suffer want and hunger; but those who seek the LORD lack no good thing." Not only does God empty us of our old selves, but He also fills us with the Holy Spirit, who is everything we need (no lack), making us entirely new creations. Our nature changes when we are delivered. Our fears change. Though we battle against self-focused fears, we are not bound to those fears because we are free to live satisfied, God-focused lives. People around us may be like ravenous lions, hungry for pleasure and control and for their selfish desires to be fulfilled because they hunger to fill a void they refuse to find in God. Christ gives God-focused fear to those who repent and turn from their sins toward God. He satisfies in ways nothing else can. The Church needs this fear; in fact, this fear defines the true Church. Anything apart from a God-focused fear needs to be seen as it truly is—self-focused fear—and eliminated quickly.

While studying to write this book, I found numerous resources on the "fear not" commands, but it was far more challenging to find insight into the "fear God" commands. Even this discovery speaks to our nature as sinners who tend to focus much more on ourselves than on God. R. C. Sproul said plainly, "We focus far too much attention on ourselves and not nearly enough on the majesty of God."[14] Consider the "fear not" commands. They encourage believers and affirm our standing before God. They relieve us of our anguish and anxiety. They are good commands, just as the command to fear God is good. But I noticed in times of trouble, I would turn to the "fear not" commands primarily for comfort. I wanted relief from my fears first and God second. In those self-focused times, I was less interested in the commands to fear God. Why? Because they place all their attention and affection on God Himself. The command to fear God is God-focused completely and ultimately. We cannot simultaneously fear other things and God, thus the command to fear God. And that is the reason we are commanded to fear God. It is a command filled with infinite blessing because, in fearing Him, we are free from all other fears—free from the power and reign of sin itself.

Distinguishing between Self-Focused and God-Focused Fear

As followers of Christ, how can we know we are living in God-focused, not self-focused, fear? The greatest litmus test for God-focused fear is how we live. Do we live according to God's Word? Do we consider the Word of God our ultimate authority on what to do and how to live? Do we submit to the truth when faced with it, or do we reject it or try to modify it to fit our preferences?

I remember my first year of teaching. My professors had prepared me well. I was confident and excited about teaching my first class of first graders.

---

[14] Sproul, R. C. 2009. *The Prayer of the Lord*. Reformation Trust Publishing.

Unfortunately, the parents had to trust that I was well-prepared and equipped to teach their children. One parent pulled her son out of my class when she learned I was a first-year teacher. Another couple was keenly aware of all I did in the classroom hoping I would challenge their daughter appropriately. No matter how good of a teacher I thought I would be, I had no proof. Even if I had the best education and training, I still needed to prove how I would perform in the classroom. Every day was either more proof that I could do what I promised as a teacher or evidence that I was falling short of expectations.

Over time the start of a new school year became less intimidating, and the first few weeks were far more enjoyable. I had those years behind me to speak for who I would be and how I would teach and care for the children in my classroom. Did that mean I gave up on my efforts to teach and care for the children well? Of course not. I continued to work toward improving each year while more people took notice. My track record spoke for me, and that was a good thing.

Similarly, Christians should waste no time proving we are the God-focused people we claim to be. Our reputations should get around quickly, and people should praise God because of His work in our lives (Matthew 5:21). Every day that goes by is another day to prove our faith. Time is a gift to us as we grow in Christ.

The reality of life in the flesh, however, is less than perfect. We know there will be hard days, and as with any lesson plan, we can prepare for it to go well, but it goes badly. We sometimes feel like we have made no progress, or the sins we commit in those hard times seem to negate everything we had worked so hard to prove about ourselves, that we belong to Christ and He is conforming us into His image. Unexpected trials come, and we fall apart. Our God-focused fear so quickly fades, and in its place are all the fears we thought we had overcome.

God knew those days would come. God knew we would constantly battle self-focused fear (sin). It isn't a struggle assigned to some and spared by others. Sin is the one and only disease that plagues every human being, without exception. God knew we had no hope of overcoming self-focused fear unless He intervened. And He did. Jesus is our only Hope.

PART II
The Gospel and the Fear of God

―――――――――― CHAPTER 7 ――――――――――

The Weight of Sin

"The saying is trustworthy and deserving of full acceptance, that Christ Jesus came into the world to save sinners, of whom I am the foremost." 1 Timothy 1:15

"People used to blush when they were ashamed. Now they are ashamed if they blush. Modesty has disappeared and a brazen generation with no fear of God before its eyes mocks at sin. We are so fond of being called tolerant and broadminded that we wink at sin when we ought to weep." Vance Havner[15]

I consider myself a decent chef. If I have a recipe to follow, the results are pretty good. As a newlywed and budding homemaker, I cooked a meal to take to friends who had recently welcomed their second baby. Though not raised in the South, I quickly became a fan of southern cuisine. I prepared them one of our favorite meals: chicken pot pie, salad, and pound cake with strawberries. I pulled out the recipe for the pound cake and followed it with care. My measurements were exact, with only one substitution. The recipe called for coarse salt, so I checked the pantry and grabbed the box of rock salt we use to make homemade ice cream. It was coarse and salt; that was all the rationale I needed. I beat the batter appropriately, poured it into the greased loaf pan, carefully placed it in the oven, and set the timer for the specified time. When I pulled it out, it looked beautiful! A few minutes after it cooled on the counter, I cut it into slices and tasted my creation like any good chef. While it looked just perfect, it tasted awful. I spit it right back out. That one teaspoon of rock salt ruined the entire pound cake. I know because I tried bites from other parts of the loaf to see if I could find at least a few decent pieces.

―――――――――――――――――――――――――――――

[15] Havner, Vance. 1984. *Day by Day with Vance Havner.* Baker Pub Group.

There were none. Shocked and so discouraged, I picked up a Sara Lee pound cake from the frozen section at our grocery store on the way to their house. My husband and I laugh about it often, but I still can't get over how that little bit of rock salt permeated the whole loaf.

Sin is the same way. We have heard it many times over. We are sinners, and our sins separate us from God. But if we really believe that, why do we care so little about our sin and its disastrous effects on our lives, the lives of those around us, and, ultimately, the testimony of Christ that others see, or don't see, in us? We focus instead on our "really good" stuff as if this will make up for our perceived little specks of bad stuff. We think all our good ingredients make up for a few bad ones, or a few bad ingredients won't do much damage, but our sins stain us apart from Christ's redeeming work in our lives. Because of this, the gospel is the only way to combat our sins. The gospel leads us to fear the LORD.

The Shift from God-Focused Fear

> "But the LORD God called to the man and said to him, 'Where are you?' And he said, 'I heard the sound of you in the garden, and I was afraid, because I was naked, and I hid myself.'" Genesis 3:9-10

God created us to be in communion with Him, to have a perfect relationship with Him and fear Him perfectly. Adam and Eve were the first to be made for that relationship. They were holy as God is holy until they sinned against God. Sin severed their perfect communion with Him at that moment because they were no longer perfect. Marred by sin, they experienced its terrible consequences—most significantly, separation from God. After they sinned, God came to them in the garden, in their sin. He called to them, but they "hid themselves from the presence of the LORD God" in shame. Replacing their perfect, God-focused fear was a sinful, self-focused fear, one that was concerned more for their punishment because of sin (servile) than mourning how their sin grieved God and separated them from Him (filial). They hid from Him because of that self-focused fear. Self-focused fear led them to disobey God as they desired to please themselves more than please Him, and self-focused fear was their response to their disobedience, hiding from God out of fear of punishment and self-preservation. This one scene shows us the reality of what happens when we move from God-focused fear to self-focused fear: separation from God.

Some may clarify it's an impossibility for Christians to be separated from God. If we have received Jesus Christ as Lord, we are with Him and will be with Him forever. Even when we sin, and we will, we will not face eternal separation. But we also know that God is holy and cannot commune with sin. Whenever we are self-focused in our words, deeds, or thoughts, we act in the flesh. We are acting in sin. Because sin cannot be in God's presence, we cease to abide in Christ each time we sin, so whenever we sin, we separate ourselves from God. He has not left us, as we are His children, but we have stepped out of communion with Him. Yes, we are ultimately forgiven for those sins if we have trusted Christ as our Savior; but every moment we act in sin, we are not abiding in Christ but living in the flesh. Only Christ Himself, who comes in the Person of the Holy Spirit, can overpower and remove the weight of sin.

Paul tells us that those who are led by the Spirit of God are sons of God and those who are in the flesh cannot please God (Romans 8). To please God as God-focused, God-fearing people, we must not only know God but allow the Spirit of God to lead us.

The Sin of Self-Willed Righteousness

> "The more serious and devoted their attempt to regain the lost image and the more proud and convincing their apparent success, the greater their contradiction to God." Dietrich Bonhoeffer[16]

Satan wanted to be God. He hated being in submission to Him, so he went his own way, falling from heaven, and living in continuous rebellion against God. He tempted Eve with this very same desire—to be like God apart from God. Instead of trusting God to reflect His image in her as He perfectly intended, she desired to work in her own efforts toward the same goal, which would forever prove fruitless.

Many of the Pharisees and religious leaders were indignant that Jesus would dare tell them that their impressive ability to "keep the law" would not save them. In their eyes, they were far more like God than Jesus and His disciples because they were "more serious and devoted" to the effort to be like

---

[16] Bonhoeffer, Dietrich. 1995. *The Cost of Discipleship*. Simon and Schuster New York.

God. But that is the hypocrisy of the Pharisees and everyone who thinks they can be like God apart from God. When we act in our own efforts, or for our own glory, we are deceived. Nothing about our self-willed actions is pleasing to God for the very reason that they are self-willed. They are not motivated by nor performed in the power of the Holy Spirit. We act exactly like the proud Pharisees, Eve, and Satan himself when we think we are more like God because of what we do on our own. We are, in fact, moving even farther away from Him with every effort of our own will.

Self-willed righteousness, or pride, leads us away from God, yet, our flesh desires it and rejects God. The world desires it and rejects God. Self-willed righteousness is contrary to true righteousness found in Christ alone. We receive true righteousness only when we confess our need for the blood of Jesus Christ to cleanse us from our unrighteousness. We are sick with sin, but even in churches, the truth that Jesus came for the sick is foreign. Many try so hard to appear well (self-willed righteousness) when the disease of sin is taking over their insides. Seeing our sin, identifying how rampant it is in our lives, and acknowledging how sick it makes us, are necessary for us to move toward God-focused fear. What is the best way to know how sick we are? To know how well we are supposed to be.

CHAPTER 8

The Significance of God Revealed

"Moses said to the people, 'Do not fear, for God has come to test you, that the fear of him may be before you, that you may not sin.'" Exodus 20:20

"God has one destined end for mankind—holiness! His one aim is the production of saints. God is not an eternal blessing-machine for men. He did not come to save men out of pity. He came to save men because He had created them to be holy." Oswald Chambers[17]

When you think about the Christian life, what words come to mind? I bet fear is not on the list. But what is likely on that list are words related to our sanctification or our progress toward holiness. As we study the fear of the LORD, we see how fearing God and our progress toward holiness are interconnected. The fear of the LORD keeps us from sin; therefore, we must be filled with the fear of the LORD to avoid sin. The verse opening this chapter illustrates the two types of fear well. It juxtaposes the wrong and right fears as Moses exhorted the Israelites soon after receiving the Ten Commandments.

God delivered Israel from Egypt three months before this terrifying scene at Mount Sinai occurred. In that dramatic rescue the people witnessed His presence in the cloud and pillar of fire, His protection from the pursuing Egyptians, His power displayed in the parting of the Red Sea, His provision in supplying for their physical needs, and His love woven through every moment of that journey. Moses, with eyes fixed on God, led the people to

---

[17] Chambers, Oswald. 2015. *My Utmost for His Highest: The Classic Daily Devotional.* Barbour Publishing.

the wilderness but for what purpose? They established camps at the base of Mount Sinai, and Moses met with God on the mountain. At that moment, God shared with Moses, as the messenger to the people, the purpose of rescuing Israel:

> "You yourselves have seen what I did to the Egyptians, and how I bore you on eagles' wings and brought you to myself. Now therefore, if you will indeed obey my voice and keep my covenant, you shall be my treasured possession among all peoples, for all the earth is mine; and you shall be to me a kingdom of priests and a holy nation." Exodus 19:4-5

God intended much greater things for them than a life in the wilderness. He meant to rescue them so they could be His treasured possession, a kingdom of priests and a holy nation, but most significantly, He saved them to bring them to Himself. He wanted to commune with them though they were sinners. The God of all creation would make them His treasured possession, but there was a weighty cost to that glorious promise—a call to obedience and keeping His covenant.

A Flippant Answer to the Call

> "If we try to obey without faith, we get nowhere. If we try to have faith without obedience, it ends in nothing." A. W. Tozer[18]

Moses came down the mountain, called all the elders, and spoke the words of God. *He has been faithful to you; He has brought you to Himself; and now He is calling you to a life of obedience. To be His treasured possession, you must obey His voice and keep His covenant.* This was the message Moses relayed to them from God. The Bible says *all* the people responded with these words: "All that the LORD has spoken we will do" (Exodus 19:8). But how could they? How could they keep all God commanded them to do? Had they not understood the gravity of what God was asking? Were they so confident in their own abilities? Did they think that obeying all God's commands would be easy? Or had they become too comfortable with God, leaning more heavily

---

[18] Tozer, A. W. 2010. *Experiencing the Presence of God: Teachings from the Book of Hebrews.* Baker Publishing Group.

on His love and grace? Surely, they knew it would be impossible to keep the covenant and obey God perfectly.

Hearing the people's response, God declared He would come to them. Hear the specific instructions God gave Moses instructing the people on how to prepare for His coming into their presence:

> "Go to the people and consecrate them today and tomorrow, and let them wash their garments and be ready for the third day. For on the third day the LORD will come down on Mount Sinai in the sight of all the people. And you shall set limits for the people all around, saying, 'Take care not to go up into the mountain or touch the edge of it. Whoever touches the mountain shall be put to death. No hand shall touch him, but he shall be stoned or shot [with arrows]; whether beast or man, he shall not live.' When the trumpet sounds a long blast, they shall come up to the mountain." Exodus 19:10-13

These were strong words. Still, Moses prepared the people accordingly. And then God came. On the morning of the third day, the thunder and lightning came first, then the thick cloud on the mountain with a thunderous trumpet blast. The people trembled in terror (Exodus 19:16). Still, Moses brought the people out of the camp to meet God as commanded. They stood at the foot of the mountain, which was "wrapped in smoke because the LORD had descended on it in fire. The smoke of it went up like the smoke of a kiln and the whole mountain trembled greatly" (Exodus 19:18). The trumpet grew louder and louder; and as it did, Moses spoke, and God answered him in thunder. What an awe-full experience that must have been.

Knowing the Israelites' interaction with God as He gave them the Ten Commandments in Exodus 20, consider this question: why descend on the mountain and terrify the people while delivering the Ten Commandments? He could have given them to Moses and Aaron to pass on to the people and skipped over that entire event. But it was necessary. Their experience with God was now fuller, weightier, and more solemn than before. God terrified them for a reason. After God gave them the Ten Commandments, and they had witnessed the thunder and flashes of lightning, the sound of the trumpet, and the mountain smoking, they were afraid and trembled (Exodus 20:18). They "stood far off" and told Moses, "You speak to us, and we will listen; but do not let God speak to us, lest we die." It was in response to this statement, when they were so afraid of the punishment of God, and they didn't even want to approach Him, that Moses spoke this powerful truth to them: "Do not fear, for God has come to test you that the fear of Him may be before you that you may not sin" (Exodus 20:20).

A Reverent Response to God's Glory

The glory of God that descended on the mountain that day overcame the Israelites. They saw His fullness, and their first response was terror. Seeing His glory was a necessary prerequisite to fearing Him. We are rightfully terrified as sinful people before a holy God when we see God as He is. God came down on Mount Sinai and showed Himself. What they saw shook them as they recognized who He was and realized the gravity of what He was asking them to do. In their forgetfulness, they had no fear before Him because they had no reason to fear Him. They forgot who they were and who He is. Others in Scripture experienced this same terror at the sight of God's glory. One of the most known passages describes how Isaiah was undone, overwhelmed by God's holiness and ashamed of his sinfulness (Isaiah 6:1-7).

The scene on Mount Sinai is one of the most terrifying images of God in the Old Testament. We see His awe-fullness. As frightening as it was, God showed His love for His people by coming down the mountain. Instead of leaving them in their ignorance, He opened their eyes to His glory. He graciously warned them through Moses. He didn't terrify them to terrorize them—He terrified them because He loved them.

Why God Came

> "Will God ever ask you to do something you are not able to do? The answer is yes—all the time! It must be that way, for God's glory and kingdom. If we function according to our ability alone, we get the glory; if we function according to the power of the Spirit within us, God gets the glory. He wants to reveal Himself to a watching world." Henry Blackaby[19]

God came down on Mount Sinai to show the Israelites Himself. Two

---

[19] Blackaby, Henry. 2009. *Experiencing the Spirit: The Power of Pentecost Every Day.* Multnomah.

thousand years ago, He came down again for the same purpose: to show us Himself. In giving us the image of the invisible God, Jesus Christ gave us a fuller picture of God's glory to warn us in love that we fall short of our holy call. But Jesus didn't come only to show us our sin. He came to make a way to bring us back to God.

God didn't come to condemn us by showing us the Law, but by showing us the Law, we know His standard and see how we fail to meet it. What makes the gospel "good news" is that God didn't leave us to fail and die in our sins but made a way for us to meet His perfect standard through faith in Jesus Christ. By His death and resurrection, Jesus paid the penalty for sin. He became sin and overcame sin so that we might become the righteousness of God when we put our trust in Him. Our obedience to God's commands is only through Christ in us, by the power of the Holy Spirit. We fail otherwise. God wants us to see our glaring failure when we see His glowing glory because recognizing our need for Him is the necessary first step to the ultimate goal of holiness. He is testing us. Any test we took in school was to assess our mastery. God tests us in the same way. He is assessing our ability to obey His voice and keep His commands. His testing proves that in our efforts, we fail every time. The goal is mastery, holiness, "that we may not sin," and the means to achieve that goal is "the fear of [God]."

Our Deliverance

Throughout Scripture God delivers His people and shows them Himself. Why is this significant? Because we often reverse the two in our minds. We think God reveals Himself to us, and then He delivers us. In truth, we cannot see Him without first being delivered. Does this contradict the earlier chapters about knowing God to fear Him? No. We are delivered so we can be with God and know Him, and then we can fear Him. Our deliverance is eternal deliverance, from eternity past to eternity future. This deliverance is our salvation.

CHAPTER 9

Salvation and Judgment

"Therefore, my beloved, as you have always obeyed, so now, not only as in my presence but much more in my absence, work out your own salvation with fear and trembling, for it is God who works in you, both to will and to work for his good pleasure." Philippians 2:12-13

"The Christian does not think God will love us because we are good, but that God will make us good because He loves us." C. S. Lewis[20]

There should be a stark contrast between those who know God through Jesus Christ and those who do not know God. The sobering truth is that the visible lines between the Church and the world are far more blurred than they should be. Sin is still raging, even in the lives of believers. The significance of our deliverance has waned, just as it did for the Israelites. Too many Christians are complacent and comfortable in habitual sins yet bank on their deliverance. But as God commanded the Israelites, bringing them to Him with a call to obedience, we too have been redeemed to obey God and please Him. Our obedience proves our deliverance. God changes our hearts through His Spirit, so we want to live as those who know and fear God. We want our lives to prove that we know Him, not because we fear the consequences, but because we are so grateful to our loving Father who loved us enough to send His only Son to die in our place. While we were still sinners, Christ died and rose again to save us so that we might, in His power and love, fear Him forever.

Through the Holy Spirit, our lives demonstrate faith in Jesus Christ, which proves our salvation. Through the Holy Spirit, we can live God-fearing

---

[20] Lewis, C. S. 2001. *Mere Christianity.* HarperOne.

lives filled with evidence of our salvation that will one day be complete. By the Holy Spirit, we produce all other necessary evidence—the fruit of the Spirit (Galatians 5:20-22). This evidence does not save us; it proves our case before a holy God.

The Judgment Seat of Christ

> "For we must all appear before the judgment seat of Christ, so that each one may receive what is due for what he has done in the body, whether good or evil." 2 Corinthians 5:10

One day we will all stand before Jesus Christ who will judge our lives. We will receive judgment for what we have done in the body. What does this have to do with the fear of God? This verse discredits the argument that how we live doesn't matter. Not only does how we live matter, but it will also be the evidence our Righteous Judge will use to determine what is due us. Everything we have ever done or will do will fall into two categories: good or evil. There will be no category for "nice try" or "so close."

What is Good?

Good is not subjective in God's eyes. Yet we often transpose our ideas of goodness on God and assume He sees goodness as we do: as a cornucopia of (subjectively) beautiful ideas, thoughts, words, and behaviors. I think any flavor of almond milk ice cream from my favorite local place is good. My husband thinks cookies and cream is the only good ice cream flavor. We appreciate our differences, as there are many. Parents think the rules they establish in their homes are good while their children may disagree with many of them. Good from the human perspective is subjective. It is hard to read verses about goodness without considering our preconceived ideas about what is good and what is not. Because our personal experiences can affect our thinking on just about any subject, from public policy to church polity, what one might think is a good thing, another might disagree. Subjectivity makes judging good and evil accurately from our perspective impossible. There must be an objective standard of goodness.

The Bible repeatedly says no one is good, no one is righteous, and no one does good and never sins (Ecclesiastes 7:20). Knowing that truth, we cannot determine what is good and what is not without objective goodness in our lives. Even as Christians who have the power of Christ in us, we do not have an automatic green light to deem our works, on our own authority, as good. But we know from God's Word that God, and only God, is good (Luke 18:19). The only Person to determine and assess what is good in every life is God Himself, and the standard He uses is His Word. Why is this important? Because we live in a world constantly shifting the goalposts for what is good and right and true. What was good many decades ago is bad now. What is right now was wrong before. The fact that God and His Word are good and unchanging should relieve the Christian because we can rely wholeheartedly on His Word as our direction for living and doing good.

Our Source of Goodness

> "As humans we have two great spiritual needs. The first is forgiveness, which God has made possible by sending His son into the world to die for our sins. Our second need, however, is for goodness, which God also made possible by sending the Holy Spirit to dwell within us." Billy Graham[21]

Not only is God the only One who determines and assesses what is good in each life, but He is also the One who empowers good in each life. We can do what God commands but with a resentful attitude or to seek our own glory. When we do that, we taint a good act with our sin. If an employee, when asked to do a job she'd rather not do, turns around and stomps off to complete the task, she may be obeying her boss externally, but in her heart there is defiance and anger. Did she obey if her heart was not working in willing submission to the request even though her hands and feet were acting as requested? I often see myself as this employee, doing the work but not yielding to the Spirit in all things. Our lives, even as Christians, are filled with sins when our heart attitude is wrong. The blessing of sanctification is that we have fewer and fewer sinful works and more and more good works in Christ. Ultimately for the Christian, the blood of Jesus Christ covers and forgives our sins—those works done in the flesh—and the good works are not ones we determine ourselves to be good from some subjective perspective. Instead, our good works are those done in the Spirit that will always be according to

---

[21] Graham, Franklin, and Donna L. Toney. 2011. *Billy Graham in Quotes*. Thomas Nelson.

God's Word. We must be keenly aware of our dependence on the Lord for everything, constantly asking, "Lord, what should I do? I need your help." Not only does He help us, He must also do the work. God's work through us is the only way we do good. My husband, Aaron, has a plaque in his office that reads, "Bear not a single care thyself, one is too much for thee. Thy work is Mine and Mine alone, thy work, to rest in Me." When we rest or abide in Christ, His work in and through us is the good and lasting fruit that pleases Him.

The Fear of God and Salvation

> "So whether we are at home or away, we make it our aim to please him." 2 Corinthians 5:9

There is no salvation without the fear of God. The only ones deserving the judgment of having done good in the body would be those who didn't do good themselves, but Christ did good in them. That also means that everyone without Christ will receive the judgment as having done evil since Christ is the only One who has ever been good. The preceding and following verses in 2 Corinthians 5 help explain why verse 9 is a necessary foundation for understanding what it means to fear God.

Fearing God pleases Him. At the end of our days, God will determine whether our lives pleased Him by how we lived or, more clearly, how Christ lived in us (Galatians 2:20). Our relationship with Jesus Christ is central to our pleasing God. Either we have a relationship with Christ and the Spirit of God dwells in us, enabling us to please God when we act in the Spirit, or we do not have a relationship with Jesus Christ, and we live in the flesh, doing evil because those who are in the flesh cannot please God (Romans 8:8-11). If fearing the LORD pleases Him and pleasing Him is only possible through His Spirit in us, which we receive through salvation, then our salvation and our fear of the LORD are inseparable.

> "Therefore, knowing the fear of the Lord, we persuade others. But what we are is known to God, and I hope it is known also to your conscience." 2 Corinthians 5:11

What we are, whether in the flesh or the Spirit, is known to God. He knows us better than we know ourselves. In the gospel of John, he tells us Jesus

Christ is the Word (John 1:1). Hebrews says, "The Word of God is living and active, sharper than any two-edged sword, piercing to the division of soul and spirit, of joints and of marrow, and discerning the thoughts and intentions of the heart" (Hebrews 4:12). Jesus is the Word of God. He is living and active in the world and our lives personally. More than any manufactured weapon, He alone can pierce through to our souls and know the thoughts and intentions of our hearts, including the status of our relationship with Him. As much as we think we know our hearts, He knows them infinitely better.

Jeremiah 17:9 warns us: "The heart is deceitful above all things, and desperately sick; who can understand it?" No one knows our hearts the way Jesus does, but this doesn't mean we constantly worry about our salvation as if we won't know until we stand before God. Paul said that he hoped the Corinthian church knew in their consciences whether they were righteous before God through Christ. So we can know in our conscience that we belong to Him. One way we know is the evidence of how we live, the fruit of the Spirit (Galatians 5:22-23). First Corinthians 5:10 says we will be judged by what we have done in the body, and verse 11 says that knowing the fear of the Lord, we persuade others. The way we live, in Christ alone and by the power of the Spirit alone, is the evidence God displays proving our salvation. It also persuades others of our salvation, and it is proof for our consciences of our salvation. Our lives lived in the Spirit are changed by the Spirit. We convince others in an argument with our lives that God is worthy of our obedience, our self-denial—our worship. Our lives, lived in the Spirit, are changed by the Spirit. The changes in our lives toward holiness, our sanctification, prove that we fear God.

CHAPTER 10

Necessary Change

"God will give ear and humble them, he who is enthroned from of old, Selah because they do not change and do not fear God." Psalm 55:19

"It is changed people who change everything. If you have been called to faith in Jesus Christ, you are part of the radically changed community, the new humanity." James Montgomery Boice[22]

We prove that we fear God by the changes toward Christlikeness in our lives. Fearing God always results in a change of heart and life toward righteousness and holiness. We can see this in two ways. First, it is a change from the old to the new. We are new creations when we are regenerated and live by the Holy Spirit (2 Corinthians 5:17). Second, we see this as a progressive change in our lives. Our understanding of this change comes from Paul's argument to the Corinthians made in an earlier part of his second letter:

> "And we all, with unveiled face, beholding the glory of the Lord, are being transformed into the same image from one degree of glory to another. For this comes from the Lord who is the Spirit." 2 Corinthians 3:18

When God gives us eyes to see the glory of Jesus Christ, we are moved from glory to glory, looking more like Christ. Our sanctification proves we fear God. When people look at our lives, they should not see us as we were ten years ago, five years ago, or even five days ago. The Spirit of God continues

---

[22] Boice, James M. 2005. *Romans: The New Humanity (Romans 12-16)*. Baker Books.

to work in us until Christ returns (Philippians 1:6). Christians yielded to the Spirit show a changed life, not simply from unbeliever to believer, but from an infant in Christ to an ever-maturing Christ-follower. The gospel makes this change possible because Christ's death for our sins and resurrection from the dead set us free from the power of sin in our own lives (Romans 8:13). His power to overcome the grave is the same power we have to overcome sin. When we believe in Christ's complete work on the cross, we receive the Spirit of God who enables us to live for righteousness (1 Peter 2:24).

Some Christians have trouble articulating the gospel beyond an intellectual explanation that includes a few verses to believe and be saved. But the gospel is more than what we can explain with words, and salvation is more than a moment of proclaimed belief. The gospel transforms us from one glory to another as much as it transfers us from the domain of darkness to the kingdom of light (Colossians 1:13). We can be so fixated on the gospel transferring us that we forget the necessary work the gospel must do to transform and conform us to the image of Christ. Our transformation by the gospel is the glory of God in us. It takes work on the part of the Spirit and yielding in our hearts to that work. When we resist that work of the Spirit, we resist the necessary change that the gospel must have in our lives. We grieve the Holy Spirit (Ephesians 4:30). When we are not willing to change or be changed, we are not fearing God but revering ourselves, certain that we know better than the Spirit. We quench that work that God wants to do when we resist or kick at the goads (1 Thessalonians 5:19, Acts 26:14).

Praising Stagnation

In recent decades, many leaders have encouraged their listeners to celebrate identities not found in Christ, even in the Christian spotlight. When we affirm others to live however they feel compelled to live, if it is contrary to God's Word, we do not love one another. Instead, we train each other to look horizontally for meaning, purpose, and identity instead of vertically. Our identity in Christ is not marked so much in a physical, external, and temporal sense. We may try to define ourselves this way, but this is the world's way. When Jesus Christ comes into our lives, He changes us from the inside out; our identity is internal and eternal—through the Spirit of God. That identity calls us out of sin and unites us with God and His people.

God loves us, even in our places of horrendous sin. But His love is not to be taken for granted. His love for us should compel us to change in the direction of godliness for His glory. We can meet one another where we are, and we must receive one another in love, but to encourage each other to remain stagnant, even in our sin, is not love. Instead of saying, "I wouldn't change one thing about you," we should encourage each other on the road to transformation. That is the God-fearing road.

When Christians use the world's language by saying, "I don't want you to change. Stay how you are if that's what you want," we promote self-focused fear with no regard for God and His commands. We communicate, "You be whoever you want to be and do not change for me or for anybody, including God and His glory;" this is not Christianity. Christianity means we will change, and we will change for the glory of God. Following Christ requires taking up our cross daily and dying to ourselves so that the life of Christ may live out in our bodies (2 Corinthians 4:10). We cannot accomplish the change; it is a work of God in our lives, but the work of change must happen, and it can happen in us because of what Christ did for us. We will honor Him even if that means giving up the way we want to live.

The Word Will Not Return Void

> "Let it never be forgotten that, although we may do nothing about the Word we hear, the Word will do something to us. The same sun melts ice and hardens clay, and the Word of God humbles or hardens the human heart." Vance Havner[23]

While change is necessary and guaranteed in a Christian, not every person will change. Many will resist the gospel's good news and insist on their way of self-focused fear, refusing to submit to Jesus Christ as Lord of their lives. Christians preach the gospel trusting God to bring others to faith in Christ, but what if they don't come to faith? What if they reject the message? These are not hypothetical questions; they are certainties. When we preach the gospel, some will come to faith, but others will reject it. Christ is either the cornerstone or the stumbling block and rock of offense (1 Peter 2:7-8).

I remember going out and sharing the gospel at conferences in high school and college. Before going, we were encouraged to faithfully share with others and not be crippled by the fact that many would turn us down. Our leaders

---

[23] Havner, Vance. 2016. *Jesus Only*. Kingsley Press.

emphasized getting the message out and being faithful to tell others the good news—a helpful perspective for me at that impressionable age when rejection was so hard to handle. If our message was rejected, it would be the gospel they rejected, not us. While offered as a means of relief, there was little comfort. They were rejecting Christ. When we speak the truth and people turn away, they are not in a battle with us, flesh against flesh, but in a spiritual war between good and evil. On one side is good, Christ and His gift of salvation sealed by the Spirit, and on the other side is evil, which is their sinful nature and its desire to rule their lives instead of Christ. But for Christians, whether it's a personal rejection or the rejection of Christ, the semantics do not change the devastation of their actions. The eternal impact of their refusal to submit to their Creator breaks our hearts.

Speaking of His Word, God says "so shall [it] be that goes out from my mouth; it shall not return to me empty (void), but it shall accomplish that which I purpose and shall succeed in the thing for which I sent it" (Isaiah 55:11). God's Word will not return to Him empty or void but will accomplish whatever purpose God intended; however, this doesn't mean when the gospel goes out, everyone will believe it. Empty, or void, is the absence of substance. So, when the gospel goes out, we know it will do something. It will serve a purpose for God. Whether received with joy or rejected, there will be a response. Paul told the Corinthians,

> "For we are the aroma of Christ to God among those who are being saved and among those who are perishing, to one a fragrance from death to death, to the other a fragrance from life to life. Who is sufficient for these things?" 2 Corinthians 2:15-16

As the Spirit changes Christians, their aroma will be undeniable. It will either be an attractive scent to the longing heart that brings them life, or a disgusting smell they revolt against and want to stay as far away from as possible. As they avoid the aroma of Christ, they continue walking the path to death. But notice Paul says, "from death to death... from life to life." The aroma of Christ, the Word Himself, will have its intended effect on every man and woman—an intended purpose that was established from before the foundations of the earth. God chose His children and those He predestined to be conformed to the image of His Son (Romans 8:29). For them, the aroma of Christ is life-giving because they have been given life in Him.

The hardest part of 2 Corinthians 2:15-16 is wrestling with the fact that others will smell the aroma of Christ and find it appalling; and in God's sovereignty, He ordained that too. We are right to mourn and grieve this truth. But we are not left to wallow in sorrow over all who reject Jesus. God grieves with us and mourns every person who denies a relationship with Him. We know this because God says, "I take no pleasure in the death of anyone… Repent and live" (Ezekiel 18:32). Scripture also tells us, "The Lord is not slow to fulfill His promise as some count slowness, but is patient toward you, not wishing that any should perish, but that all should reach repentance" (2 Peter 3:9).

How can the Lord wish that all might repent and yet still sovereignly rule over who does and does not turn to Him? I believe this is a question with depth far beyond the wisdom He has given humanity for now, but we know this much: these two truths can co-exist, or God would not have said it. Jesus has not come back because God is patient with us and all of humanity. How can He be patient or long-suffering unless there is more to do? What needs to be done? More must "reach repentance"—the destination for those God calls.

For some, initial repentance comes after hearing the gospel for the first time. Others hear the gospel and reject it twenty times but hear it that twenty-first time, "reach repentance," and believe. For the person who repented the first time or the twenty-first time, the aroma of Christ was "life to life" because God had that moment in mind from eternity past to open their eyes, give them a new heart, and make them a new creation. No matter how many times they rejected it before, it only takes the Holy Spirit one time to regenerate a life (Titus 3:5). He enters once, but His work is ongoing.

The Subtle Rejection

Seeing the Spirit's sanctifying work in others' lives may cause some who grew up in church to wonder, "I have not rejected the message of the gospel, but I don't think I have experienced that change of heart or that maturing to be more like Jesus through the power of the Holy Spirit." It may not seem like it, but this acknowledgment could be a subtle rejection that is not as overt as the world's rejection. Left unchecked it can still be disastrous because people have accepted the truth of the gospel but refuse to let it change their lives. The devil thrives on this quiet and subtle rejection by churchgoers because it serves his agenda while leading them down a destructive path.

The devil prowls around like a roaring lion seeking to devour, and his favorite stomping ground is churches. He uses people who subtly and quietly resist the Spirit to try to destroy the Church (impossible) and ruin its testimony to the world (not only possible but currently happening). Those who quietly continue to reject the Spirit—consistently turning from Him—are acting as wolves in sheep's clothing (Matthew 7:15). Though they claim to love the aroma of Christ, they hate it but don't want to tell people that. They are filled with bitterness and jealousy as they watch people in the Church living in the power of the Holy Spirit. They are ravenous wolves who long for that righteousness but keep striving for it in their own power. Their rage leads them to destroy instead of uniting in Christ and Him crucified.

Is there hope for those who recognize the devil's strongholds in their lives? Is there a chance for the one who says, "I have been that person; I have yearned for the righteousness and peace I see in others; I have tried to destroy relationships instead of uniting with others in Christ, but I want to change?" Praise God, yes! The Lord is patient for that one as He has been patient with each of His children thus far. The apostle Paul was that person and everyone who turns to Christ comes from that same place of humble admission of the wretchedness of our sin. The aroma of Christ, which we used to revile against, is now a sweet and satisfying aroma that moves us from life to life through the work of the Spirit. This "reaching repentance" is what He patiently waits for in all His children. And once we reach repentance, we don't check it off the task list; that is where we live. That place of repentance is where the Christian remains. It becomes our posture before God.

CHAPTER 11

Forgiveness, Repentance, and Reconciliation

"For God so loved the world, that he gave his only Son, that whoever believes in him should not perish but have eternal life. For God did not send his Son into the world to condemn the world, but in order that the world might be saved through him." John 3:16-17

"God proved his love on the Cross. When Christ hung, and bled, and died, it was God saying to the world, 'I love you.'" Billy Graham[24]

Some things are easier said than done. Forgiveness is one of those things. I remember some friends hurt me deeply, and I struggled. Months after the offense, I attended a conference and went to a breakout session on forgiveness. I walked into the session broken and mad, with a heart that wasn't ready but a mind that knew what God wanted me to do. Scripture mandates that we forgive one another. There are no exceptions. This truth broke my heart even more as I grieved what happened and my resisting heart. But at the same time, I wanted them to apologize and repent of their wrongs done against me. With the relationships broken, I was wrestling with step one: forgiveness.

Our relationships with one another can parallel our relationship with God in many ways, both good and bad. And they often model our heart's understanding of God's commands. Healthy relationships usually reflect a proper understanding of God's commands and show external proof of hearts willing to obey Him. In contrast, unhealthy relationships often reflect either a wrong

---

[24] Graham, Billy. 1966. *The Quotable Billy Graham.* 1st ed. Droke House.

idea of God's commands or resistance to obeying Him. Since that conference, I have had more conflicts in relationships. In my own experiences as the offender and the offended, I have learned that many Christians, myself included, have misunderstood or resisted forgiveness, repentance, and reconciliation. Because of this confusion or rejection, congregations are handicapped in their relationships with God and others, making it impossible to fear Him. God desires us to have a right relationship with Him and one another, but we must apply His understanding of forgiveness, repentance, and reconciliation.

Forgiveness

The focus of the session I attended was a most significant truth we forget or deny regarding forgiveness—forgiving others can be accomplished without involving others; it is a work in the heart of the offended and doesn't require the offender's request or approval. I spent most of my life, mainly those childhood years with my brother doing the whole "I'm sorry I did that. Will you forgive me?" "It's ok. Yes, I forgive you." This scripted conversation, likely familiar to all, is helpful as it shows us the necessity of forgiveness; but it can be misleading too. It can make us think the offender must participate in accomplishing forgiveness. We don't have to wait for offenders to repent before we can forgive; God commands us to forgive regardless of whether they ask.

The Lord's prayer includes a cry to God to "forgive us our debts, as we also have forgiven our debtors" (Matthew 6:12). The forgiveness we give to others and our own forgiveness intertwine. In the verses immediately following that prayer, Jesus warns: "If you do not forgive others their trespasses, neither will your Father forgive your trespasses" (Matthew 6:15). If our forgiveness of others were contingent on their involvement in the process, then we would be blamed for the failure to forgive even if we were obedient to forgive in our own hearts. Instead, we can forgive without being bound to another's response or behavior. With that freedom comes responsibility. We are accountable to God for our willingness and obedience to forgive as He has forgiven us. We cannot stand before God and say, "I couldn't forgive them because they never came to me and apologized," or "they never changed their behavior, so I couldn't completely forgive them." No. While we were still sinners, God forgave our debts through Christ's death on the cross (Romans 5:8). God wanted a right relationship with us enough to send His only Son to die on the cross, not after we repented, but before. When we forgive as God forgave us, before the offender comes in repentance, we are saying, "I love you and want to have a right relationship with you. I am ready for that right relationship when you are"—this is what God in Christ did for us.

Forgiveness Doesn't Guarantee Reconciliation

Another point of clarification we often overlook is that forgiveness is the foundation for a restored relationship, but it doesn't guarantee one. Forgiveness is the hope of reconciliation but not the guarantee. True reconciliation is impossible when two individuals offend each other, and one forgives, but the other individual refuses to forgive. In other cases, the offended can forgive, but the offenders may not see their offense or refuse to repent, making a right and healthy relationship difficult, if not impossible. In these situations, forgiveness can occur, yet the relationship is still not rightly restored.

Forgiving those not seeking forgiveness who choose to remain in sin raises an interesting question: Can God do the same thing? Scripture is clear: "God so loved the world," "Christ died once for all," and "He is the propitiation… for the sins of the whole world" (John 3:16, 1 Peter 3:18, 1 John 2:2). The blood of Christ, the perfect Lamb, was shed for the forgiveness of sins. If the command is to forgive everyone, wouldn't that only be possible if God in Christ has done it first? Otherwise, how could He enable us to do what He cannot do Himself?

Think of Christ's words on the cross. When He hung on the cross bearing the weight of the sins of the world, He said, "Father, forgive them, for they know not what they are doing" (Luke 23:34). Can we argue that Jesus, who is perfect, prayed an imperfect prayer on the cross, one that was contrary to God the Father's will since God did not save all men who murdered Him? If Christ only died for the sins of the elect, how could he pray to the Father to "forgive them," many of whom never believed? Or could it be that in Christ's death on the cross, He was forgiving them? What if He was praying and answering His prayer simultaneously? I am not suggesting that Christ's death on the cross accomplished salvation for all, but it was the propitiation for the sins of the world, opening the door for a reconciled relationship with God for anyone who would confess their sins and believe Christ's redemptive work on the cross. If we can forgive someone and not have a reconciled relationship with them because they resist or refuse, then can God not also forgive the sins of the whole world yet not reconcile those to Himself who, in His sovereignty, reject Him?

The Vital Role of Repentance

> "The chief danger that confronts the coming century will be religion without the Holy Ghost, Christianity without Christ, forgiveness without repentance..." William Booth[25]

With all the weight put on forgiveness in today's Christian culture, we think forgiveness is all it takes to have a right relationship with God and others. "God loves us unconditionally," we hear. No matter how much we sin, He forgives us, but that forgiveness only leads to reconciliation with God when we meet Him in sorrow over our sins (repentance). Too often, forgiveness happens without reconciliation because there's a lack of repentance.

Many of the minor prophets, John the Baptist, and Jesus Himself proclaimed a very different message than the one we hear today. Today the message is: "Come to God, and He will love you no matter what." Their message was "Repent!" We distort the gospel message if we remove repentance from the equation. Forgiveness does not equal reconciliation; reconciliation is the sum of forgiveness and repentance. We must take ownership of our sin. It is the only thing we bring to the table; unless we admit our sins to God with repentant hearts, He will not remove them. Still, today's religious world has nearly eliminated repentance by promoting a relationship with God that doesn't require us to sacrifice anything, including—and especially—our sins. Many do not fear the consequences of living *in* their sins, so they continue to live with no repentance *of* their sins. But the gospel is incomplete in our lives without repentance.

True Repentance

> "True repentance is firm and constant, and makes us war with the evil that is in us, not for a day or a week, but without end and without intermission." John Calvin[26]

Repentance is more than a simple confession or acknowledgment of our sins. We can verbally acknowledge our sins without grieving them and

---

[25] Dempster, Stephen G. 2017. *Micah: The Two Horizons Old Testament Commentary*. Wm. B. Eerdmans Publishing Company.
[26] Calvin, John . 1849. *Tracts Relating to the Reformation, Volume 2*. Calvin Translation Society.

confess them without a desire to change toward righteousness. "Thousands acknowledge they are sinners, who have never mourned over the fact."[27] True repentance is sorrow over our sins and a desire to change by God's power and for His glory. If the goal is not a changed heart, it is not repentance. Some might argue, "What about Scripture that tells us to confess our sins and He will be faithful and just to forgive us our sins and cleanse us from all unrighteousness" (1 John 1:9)? We must consider the heart behind the confession. Are we self-focused: confessing because we were caught, because the optics look good and humble, or because it checks the necessary box? Or, are we God-focused in confessing because of our brokenness from sinning against a holy God and we desire to please Him and bring Him glory?

When we repent, we receive God's mercies. Because of Christ's death the sins we grieve and mourn over are gone; as far as the east is from the west, God removes them (Psalm 103:12). There is no condemnation for those in Christ (Romans 8:1). We are free from the penalty of sin and the power of sin in our lives. We can rejoice in all of this but at the same time remember from where we came. Remembering our forgiven sins and waking up to His new mercies gives us hearts of gratitude that long to extend the same grace and mercy of God to others. The Holy Spirit can help us offer mercy to all, even our greatest enemy, every day. We don't know what impact our kindness and forgiveness may have on them. The tangible demonstration of Christ's love for them in our forgiveness and kindness toward them may be what He uses to bring them to eternal glory with Himself.

Completing the Transaction

Forgiveness lays the foundation for reconciliation in our relationship with God and each other. It is essential and cannot work in isolation. Each component (forgiveness, repentance, and reconciliation) is necessary to understand the gospel and salvation. God has forgiven us through Jesus Christ, but we must receive His forgiveness. To receive His forgiveness, we must acknowledge we need it (repentance). We must admit our sins against God and express our grief. We can sit in bitterness, resentment, and self-loathing, but we will not receive the forgiveness we need until we come

---

[27] Pink, Arthur W. 2011. *An Exposition of the Sermon on the Mount.* Bottom of the Hill Publishing.

to the cross with repentant hearts. We can only find it at the cross, and we must go with broken hearts, ready to meet the One who has already forgiven us. When we come to Christ repenting of our sins and receiving His forgiveness, reconciliation occurs, and the glorious transaction of our sin for His righteousness is complete. In these moments, holy gravity does its work.

Reconciliation with God happens initially when we receive the gift of faith by grace; but we are also reconciled in right communion with God every time we see our sin and turn from it day after day, hour after hour. When we do what we don't want to do or don't do what we want to do, we act in the flesh and do not abide in the Spirit. Given eyes to see our sin, we can repent, confess, and be restored to communion with God by the Spirit or remain in our sin. The ministry of reconciliation is ongoing in the life of the believer, between the believer and God, and believers with one another (2 Corinthians 5:18-21). As the Spirit helps us apply God's right understanding of forgiveness and repentance in our relationships with Him and others, we can experience the ministry of reconciliation every day. In this place of restored, right communion with God and each other, we can live holy lives that fear Him. For the rest of the book, we will study how the Spirit manifests the fear of the LORD in the lives of His people through wisdom, love, obedience, and suffering.

PART III
Wisdom and the Fear of God

CHAPTER 12

The Beginning of Wisdom

"The fear of the LORD is the beginning of wisdom, and the knowledge of the Holy One is understanding." Proverbs 9:10 (NASB)

"I do not even want religion to define God for me. I want the Holy Spirit to reveal God to me." A. W. Tozer[28]

How important are beginnings? A novel would make little sense if we started in the middle. If we start a marathon from our house instead of the designated beginning, we can expect a disqualification from the race. Enrolling our children in school for the first time as middle schoolers without the beginning educational training of kindergarten ensures failure. And we can't build a house starting with the roof; we need to lay the foundation first.

The Bible starts with, "In the beginning..." and Proverbs tells us that the fear of the LORD is the beginning of wisdom. Beginnings are essential and we must understand their role in every process. The examples above show us that the beginning is not just a stepping stone to something better. The beginning is the foundation for the whole experience. As wisdom relates to the fear of God, Solomon makes a similar statement. It's not that wisdom is more important than fearing God, as if the fear of God is only step one, and then we move on to other things. He recognizes the fear of the LORD as the foundation upon which wisdom is built. Without the fear of God, there can be no wisdom. And to grow in wisdom, we must begin and remain in the fear of the LORD. The fear of God is the foundation for wisdom, the groundwork for a life of wisdom.

---

[28] Tozer, A. W. 2013. *God's Power for Your Life: How the Holy Spirit Transforms You Through God's Word.* Regal.

We Need Wisdom

Remembering what we have already learned about the fear of God, there is a necessary self-awareness that propels us into a right, God-focused fear. Knowing that we lack wisdom is essential to fearing God and is key to accessing His wisdom. When we recognize who we are apart from God, we are not only overwhelmed by our sinfulness (manifested in our foolish attempts to live by our own wisdom), but we also acknowledge our Holy God's right to judge us for sin. This knowledge is God's wisdom given to those who are willing to see the truth. When we see ourselves rightly as those who need God's wisdom, and if we want to bring Him honor and glory, then we can know God, and all the riches of His wisdom can flow from Him through us. If we deny who we are apart from God, sinners with no capacity to do good or please Him, then we don't see any need for Him in our lives. If we don't see a need for Him, we don't have access to His power and wisdom. "Pride leads to disgrace, but with humility comes wisdom" (Proverbs 11:2).

The world tells us we don't need God. They say we can be wise without the only wise God (Jude 25). They say we can navigate difficult waters without Him, the only One who knows the future and the right way to go (Isaiah 46:10). They say we can care for ourselves better than He can, the only one who perfectly loves (1 Chronicles 16:34). But the world is not alone in telling us these lies. Our flesh tells us the same thing. Every day, whether we are faithful to attend church or stay thousands of miles away from one, we all have the same sinful nature to battle against every day. The wisdom of our flesh tells us to believe in ourselves more, listen to ourselves more, trust ourselves more. Our response to these lies and temptations separates the wise from the foolish. Do we believe our own wisdom and the wisdom of the world, or do we believe the wisdom of God?

God's Wisdom vs. Our Wisdom

> "Trust in the LORD with all your heart, and do not lean on your own understanding. In all your ways acknowledge him and he will make straight your paths. Be not wise in your own eyes; fear the LORD and turn away from evil." Proverbs 3:5-7

The wise trust in the Lord with an undivided heart. Their faith is in Him alone and they do not trust in their own understanding. As finite people, we do not have infinite knowledge or understanding of anything, so to trust in our own understanding apart from God's wisdom is foolish. This verse's exhortation to trust the Lord doesn't only relate to life decisions or struggles, like choosing a college or dealing with a conflict at work. We often read Proverbs 3:5-6 and remind ourselves not to depend on our understanding of the situation but to trust the Lord for His good guidance in our lives. While an excellent reminder to trust Him in social and personal issues, we should equally trust Him for all spiritual truth and understanding. Solomon follows with verse 7 to remind us again not to depend on our own wisdom but to fear the LORD and, consequently, shun evil.

We must realize our own understanding can seep into our perceptions of God and His Word. Christians are not immune to the temptation to lean on our own understanding. We can still fall prey to tunnel vision with binoculars focused on our own wisdom, even regarding our views of God and His Word. The results are obvious. We have false teachings and unhealthy interpersonal relationships in our churches that prove people lack the understanding that comes from God through His Spirit. When we trust God's wisdom and reject our own, the Spirit helps us walk a straight and righteous path, shunning evil.

Knowledge and Understanding

> "And he said to man, 'Behold, the fear of the Lord, that is wisdom, and to turn away from evil is understanding.'" Job 28:28

"Wise people are smart people," we think. But is wisdom not much more than intellect? While wise people do have a great deal of knowledge, what makes them wise is the good and right application of that knowledge. The knowledge of God Himself, the foundation of godly wisdom, leads to a good and right application of that knowledge in a person's life (understanding). James tells us the wise and understanding among us can be identified by their "good conduct" as they show their works in the meekness of wisdom (James 3:13). God-focused fear leads to a life of wisdom demonstrated by our conduct.

We cannot fear God if we don't know Him because in knowing Him, we have the ability to fear Him. Solomon ties this truth into our understanding of the fear of the LORD when he says, "knowledge of the Holy One is understanding." This knowledge is different than strictly a mental recognition of something. The word "knowledge" in this verse is the same word Paul used speaking to the church in Colossae. He speaks of his ministry to the church and why he struggled so faithfully for them. He does so "that their hearts may be encouraged, being knit together in love, to reach all the riches of full assurance of understanding and the knowledge of God's mystery, which is Christ, in whom are hidden all the treasures of wisdom and knowledge" (Colossians 2:2).

Wisdom is the product of knowing Christ, and this knowledge comes through His Holy Spirit. Christ is the means through which we gain assurance of understanding because all the treasures of wisdom and knowledge are in Him. In Him, we can "reach all the riches of full assurance of understanding." What is this full assurance of understanding? It is the Holy Spirit's application of our knowledge of God. This knowledge in Christ compels us to apply what we know.

Consider how children show their understanding in school. They apply their knowledge in various situations, whether it be classwork, homework, tests, quizzes, or helping teach other children the concepts they have come to know. The teacher knows the children who understand because they prove that understanding by completing the tasks correctly and passing the tests. The same is true for Christians—we prove our understanding of God, our wisdom in Christ, through our work in the Spirit, by the things we do and say that please Him, and by turning away from evil (sin). This knowledge and understanding are only possible because of Christ in us. Wisdom is not a state of mental elitism but an active way of life as we demonstrate our fear of God by living holy lives in Him.

Wisdom and the Gospel

> "For Christ did not send me to baptize but to preach the gospel, and not with words of eloquent wisdom, lest the cross of Christ be emptied of its power. For the word of the cross is folly to those who are perishing, but to us who are being saved it is the power of God... And because of [God] you are in Christ Jesus, who became to us wisdom from God, righteousness and sanctification and redemption..." 1 Corinthians 1:17-18, 30

The gospel is God's wisdom and the cross its power. When we receive this message in our hearts, we have access through Christ to God's wisdom and power; this compels us to live and tell the good news. Believing the truth of the gospel doesn't guarantee we will live righteously and choose God's wisdom every moment of every day. Paul explains in Romans the battle between the Spirit and the flesh is one we will endure until we die or Christ returns. Christians still battle the flesh which means we battle our own wisdom, our confidence in that wisdom, and our temptation to give in to it when it contradicts God's wisdom. We can do this even when we share the gospel with others, leaning too much on our eloquent words or academic brilliance. Paul warns that we can empty the cross of its power because what should be done in God-focused fear, leading others to love and fear Him, becomes a work of self-focused fear as we draw people to ourselves instead of God. If we strive in our own wisdom to speak more eloquently than truthfully and lovingly, we fail to put the emphasis in the only right place. Wisdom and power are found in Christ alone and as messengers, we have no authority to elaborate or alter the gospel message, nor do we have the right to make the message about the messenger. If we do any of those things, we risk emptying the cross of its power because, in our own wisdom, we put faith in man's approach to salvation instead of in God's authority and power to save.

The early church, driven by Christ's wisdom and power after receiving the Holy Spirit, preached the gospel alone and many were added to their number (Acts 2:41, 2:47). Their focus was the cross of Christ; it was the power that came from the message of the cross that saved. Peter's sermon at Pentecost is a persuasive example of the word of the cross being the power of God for salvation (Acts 2:14-41). In his example, the greatest source of power to save is the truth and we find that truth in God's Word.

Wisdom and Salvation

> "[From] infancy you have known the Holy Scriptures, which are able to make you wise for salvation through faith in Christ Jesus." 2 Timothy 3:15 (NIV)

The world needs salvation that only Jesus Christ can offer. They need the truth and Christians have that truth. We have truth within us, and we hold it in our hands—the Bible. Paul highlighted for Timothy the significance of knowing God's Word. Paul rightly valued Scripture knowing it all points to Jesus Christ who is our wisdom and salvation.

The Berean Jews received Paul and Silas in the synagogues as they taught them that Jesus is the Christ. "[They] received the word with all eagerness, examining the Scriptures daily to see if these things were so." The Bereans didn't simply take Paul and Silas at their word; they checked their words against Scripture to see if they were true. They were not passive listeners but active studiers. And the results proved their study was well worth the effort: "Many of them *therefore* believed, with not a few Greek women of high standing as well as men" (Acts 17:12). Because they searched the Scriptures, the Lord opened their eyes to see the truth and believe, and well-respected Gentiles around them believed too. God promises when we seek Him with our whole hearts, we will find him (Jeremiah 29:13). The Bereans were proof of that promise. They were willing to put in the work of study and question their understanding to know the truth.

The Church is weak today because we know little of God's Word. Our weakness makes us easy prey for the devil to lure us away from God since we are most susceptible to the devil's lies when we don't know the truth. The Bible is a precious, life-giving gift from God that can make us wise for salvation through faith in Christ. When we read it, study it, and meditate upon it, it changes us because it is living and active (Hebrews 4:12). It convicts us and sanctifies us because the Word has the power to save both instantly and progressively. If we believe God's Word can make us wise for salvation from our sins, we will raise it to the highest place in our hearts and minds. We would seek to know it better than we know anything else. And when we know it, we don't just know any old book: "In the beginning was the Word, and the Word was with God and the Word was God" (John 1:1). We know the Beginning who is our foundation.

CHAPTER 13

The Significance of Scripture

"Come, O children, listen to me; I will teach you the fear of the LORD." Psalm 34:11

"The Bible was not given for our information but for our transformation." D. L. Moody[29]

If our highest call is to love God, our highest responsibility is to know Him. He wants to reveal Himself to us if we only take the time to seek Him. When we do, we grow in our fear of Him. God calls us to come to Him. He doesn't force us, but bids us come. He calls children to come, not only in age but in heart, dependent and willing to hear and learn from Him. It is God who teaches us the fear of the LORD. He uses many vessels and vehicles to do it, but He is the only One who can teach us what it means to fear Him. So, we must diligently seek to know Him; the best way to do that is through His Word.

The State of Theology

> "Theology means the study of God; and if we are to love God as we are commanded, with all our 'minds,' then we need to be in the business of theology." J. I. Packer[30]

Every two years, Ligonier Ministries and LifeWay Research conduct a survey among Americans to learn about trends in our understanding and

---

[29] Source unknown
[30] "Interview with J. I. Packer." Modern Reformation, July/August 1993.

belief about God, the Person and work of Jesus Christ, the inerrancy of Scripture and other core principles of Christianity. Our world desperately needs the truth, but this survey proves even evangelicals are confused about the truth. One of the most shocking responses in the 2022 survey came from the following statement: "Jesus was a great teacher, but he was not God." While Scripture teaches that Jesus is God, almost half of U.S. evangelicals reject the deity of Christ. Among U.S. Evangelicals, 43% agreed with the statement, an incredible 13% jump from responses to the same question only two years prior. Here are some other key trends identified in their 2022 survey:

- Almost two-thirds of U.S. evangelicals, 65%, believe "everyone is born innocent in the eyes of God;" this is only six percentage points below the same question asked of all U.S. adults, in which case, 71% agreed with the same statement.
- One quarter, 26%, of U.S. evangelicals believe "the Bible, like all sacred writings, contains helpful accounts of ancient myths but is not literally true."
- Over one-third, 38%, of American evangelicals think religious belief is a matter of personal opinion; it is not about objective truth. "A rising disbelief in the Bible's literal truth may help us understand why American evangelicals also increasingly believe that religious faith is a subjective experience rather than an objective reality."[31]

These results, while devastating, are not surprising. By neglecting the study of God's Word, we miss opportunities for the Spirit to reveal truth to us and we find ourselves lost and confused. These missed opportunities over time can become seasons of drought, discouragement, doubt, and despair. If our neglect of God's Word continues, the damage is no longer individual but societal, and these seasons can compound into decades of major cultural shifts away from the Lord, who is truth and wisdom and whose Holy Spirit imparts an understanding of the truth that changes our lives. If we are willing to study and submit to the Word, the Lord will change us, and cultures around us can be transformed by Him too.

---

[31] "The State of Theology." The State of Theology. Ligonier Ministries and LifeWay Research, September 22, 2022.

Bible Reading Trends

The State of the Bible serves as another helpful resource for learning about Americans' relationships with the Bible, faith, and the Church. The American Bible Society and the Barna Study Group publish an annual State of the Bible report. Between 2018 and 2021 Americans' engagement with the Bible was moving in a promising direction. According to the 2021 results, "one in six U.S. adults (16%)… [read] the Bible most days during the week—up from one in eight (12%) in 2020."[32]

The survey groups Americans into three categories: Bible Disengaged, Movable Middle, and Scripture Engaged. While the Bible Disengaged group dropped progressively from 136 million to 100 million between 2018 and 2021, this same group dramatically increased to 145 million from 2021 to 2022. "In 2022, the trend toward Bible exploration came to an abrupt end. The Moveable Middle [fell] by two in five and the Scripture Engaged category [shrank] by one in five."[33] These results numerically represent what we are experiencing in American culture today. The less we read and know God's Word, the more sin infests our lives and communities. We need the truth to restore all the brokenness we see in our world, yet we aren't looking to truth for His wisdom and power to restore and heal. Naturally, we can expect the results to be decay and destruction. There is no fear of God in the land.

We have many anemic churches in America. We are malnourished. We are studying the world and each other far more than we are studying Scripture and yielding to the Spirit's work in our lives through it. Prioritizing our study this way results in weakness, not strength. Our lack of understanding, based on the assessment of our application, is evident. When we recognize the value of God's Word and how it serves to teach us, reprove us, correct us, and train us in righteousness, we cannot be indifferent to it.

Study vs. Meditation

> "What is the best safeguard against false teaching? Beyond all doubt the regular study of the word of God, with prayer for the teaching of the Holy Spirit." J. C. Ryle[34]

---

[32] "State of the Bible." State of the Bible. American Bible Society, April 6, 2022.
[33] "State of the Bible." 2022. American Bible Society. Retrieved from http://sotb.research.bible.
[34] Ryle, J. C. 1986. *Expository Thoughts on the Gospels: Matthew.* Banner of Truth.

In the book *Celebration of Discipline*, Richard Foster explains the significance of spiritual disciplines in our lives. He exhorts us to prioritize our relationship with the Lord through obedience in the form of these disciplines. In his chapter about study, he compares meditation and the study of the Bible. "Meditation is devotional; study is analytical. Meditation will relish a word; study will explicate it."[35] Meditation is continued pondering of a word, verse, or passage of Scripture and study develops a spiritual truth beyond its face value. Study aims to understand it better by seeking out other passages in Scripture that address the same topic or include a similar root word.

Both meditation and study are helpful and vital for believers. We know Mary pondered the things she learned in her heart, and the Bereans searched the Scriptures, noting just one example of each. While they are both beneficial, we can easily neglect to study the Bible, promoting meditation primarily through devotional books. Our fast-paced culture has elevated devotional books to a dangerously high position. There can be great value in these books supplementally, but the disadvantage is that they cripple our ability to study the truths ourselves. We may learn more about God and delight in His Word, but we don't work hard for it. The author of the devotional has done the work of study. We read it and glean truth from it without much effort on our part. We become dependent on the secondhand teaching of God's Word, so we don't even bother with firsthand study, during which the Spirit can reveal profound truths we had not known before. If we aren't willing to sacrifice our time to know God better, how can we be sure we will sacrifice anything else for Him?

We live in a society that loves the easy way—whatever is less work for us. We have a lot to do, so we choose the most efficient option. The world has trained us, even in churches, to seek efficiency over effectiveness. Churches are embracing this ease of life instead of fighting against it. We are too busy for Bible study. Our busyness has proven to be a great threat to the Church. It has forced us out of studying God's Word, and for the sake of time and efficiency, we look for easy ways to meditate on it. However, the risk of meditation without study is that we don't know if we are meditating on right and true things.

Personal study of God's Word is our safeguard against false teaching. The Spirit enlightens us, gives us understanding, and directs us to others passages

---

[35] Foster, Richard. 2018. *Celebration of Discipline, Special Anniversary Edition: The Path to Spiritual Growth*. HarperOne.

of Scripture that confirm the truths we are coming to know. If we do not know Scripture through diligent study, we cannot refute false teaching, and we are far more susceptible to believing lies instead of the truth. Yes, study requires work, but all good treasures do. The most precious stones lie deep but are always worth the digging. God is our great Treasure, and He wants us to seek Him. He wants us to know Him and become more like Him with every dig of the shovel.

The Call to Maturity

> "For though by this time you ought to be teachers, you need someone to teach you again the basic principles of the oracles of God. You need milk not solid food, for everyone who lives on milk is unskilled in the word of righteousness, since he is a child. But solid food is for the mature, for those who have their powers of discernment trained by constant practice to distinguish good from evil." Hebrews 5:12-14

With our busy schedules, we often talk about tips for squeezing in time with God and ways to meditate on Scripture. These are real struggles. I remember seasons when meditating on God's Word was sparse and studying it was nearly non-existent. I don't deny the reality of these challenges, but the challenges don't excuse us from seeking what God wants most from us—a deep and abiding relationship with Him.

We can grow in our knowledge and understanding of God through meditation, but we cannot fully develop. Our growth stunts without in-depth and Spirit-led study of Scripture. Studying God's Word changes us because we meet with Him when we study. We are not hearing about Him secondhand but experiencing Him firsthand. Through studying His Word, He renews our minds. He matures us through testing. He disciplines us so we can teach others. If we don't study the Bible, longing for and digesting its hearty truth, we cannot progress. As the writer of Hebrews explained, his listeners should have been farther along than they were but they needed someone to teach them. They still required milk because they couldn't handle solid food. Paul said something similar to the Corinthian church: "I fed you with milk, not solid food, for you were not ready for it. And even now you are not yet ready" (1 Corinthians 3:2). Although we should be farther along, we find ourselves drinking the same milk for years, in some cases, decades. When this happens, we are not prepared for the harder truths (solid food) of Scripture that might choke us instead of strengthening us. Conversely, as we develop through faithful study of Scripture, we grow in wisdom, we grow up in maturity, sanctification, and Christlikeness.

Wisdom from One Shepherd

> "The words of the wise are like goads, and like nails firmly fixed are the collected sayings; they are given by one Shepherd. My son, beware of anything beyond these. Of making many books there is no end, and much study is a weariness of the flesh." Ecclesiastes 12:11-12

In the final chapter of Ecclesiastes, Solomon gives us a profound warning about finding true wisdom. He tells us One Shepherd gives the words of the wise and the collected sayings. The wise among us do not teach their own wisdom but teach what is given to them by the One Shepherd, Jesus Christ. They teach us from His unchanging, "firmly fixed" Word. Solomon warns, "beware of anything beyond these." The trouble we find ourselves in today is that many teachers are going beyond the Word of God and adding to the gospel. They tell others salvation is through believing Christ and ____ or believing Christ except for ____. They may even deny the deity of Jesus Christ, reject the Trinity, or claim salvation through a completely alternate route. All these statements or beliefs twist the wisdom given by our One Shepherd. If we are to recognize this false teaching, we must know our Shepherd and the words He speaks. We must study the Word.

Solomon continues by saying there is no end to new books. The irony is not lost on me that I sit writing another book to add to the world's abundant collection. But the gravity of Solomon's words ground me. If any part of this book tries to go beyond the Word of God in any way, aiming to add, edit, or omit, it is wrong and worthless content. If, however, the words in this book come from One Shepherd, and are founded on His Word alone, they have eternal value and significance because they come from Him.

Solomon's final words in these verses warn that "much study is weariness of the flesh." There is a right study of God's Word and a wrong study. The right study results in a growing fear of God and the wrong study leaves us wanting. Writing books and studying to write books have a good purpose, especially as we seek to edify and build up the body (Ephesians 4:11-13). Still, the intellectuals among us must tread so carefully. Our study of God's Word should not press us toward a fleshly work lacking the wisdom that comes from Christ and the application of that knowledge through the power of the Spirit. The motive of our study should be to know the One Shepherd and know His way so that we may walk in it by His power. As we learn God's way we can yield to His life-changing work in our lives.

CHAPTER 14

Discernment

"Whoever is wise, let him understand these things; whoever is discerning, let him know them; for the ways of the LORD are right, and the upright walk in them, but transgressors stumble in them." Hosea 14:9

"If you would test the character of anything, you only need to inquire whether that thing leads you to God or away from God." Watchman Nee[36]

Life is not black and white, but everything in life is black or white. There is right and wrong, light and darkness, and good and evil. The challenge is knowing the truth in every situation.

Discernment is not a simple formula like 2+2=4. It is far more complex than appearances and external criteria. We live in a wicked world, surrounded by sinners; we have an enemy on the prowl, wolves in sheep's clothing, and our own sinful hearts deceive us. Clouded by our selfish preferences and desires, we see what we want to see instead of what God sees; too many times, things are not what they seem. What appears good and true may be corrupt. One clear example of this truth comes in Paul's warning that Satan disguises himself as an angel of light (2 Corinthians 11:14). And what we deem wrong could be right, considering our conscience vs. the conscience of another (1 Corinthians 8). If we aren't careful, we can be easily led astray, so we must ask God for discernment.

In these days of great confusion and deception, we must be vigilant, soberminded, and completely dependent on God. Discernment is impossible apart

---

[36] Nee, Watchman. 1994. *The Collected Works of Watchman Nee*. Living Stream Ministry.

from His Spirit. We can diligently study God's Word, but if we are not yielded to the Spirit's work in our heart through that study, abiding in Him, we will lack discernment in all areas of life. "The natural person does not accept the things of the Spirit of God, for they are folly to him, and he is not able to understand them because they are spiritually discerned" (1 Corinthians 2:14).

Discerning Spiritual Truth

> "But the anointing that you received from him abides in you, and you have no need that anyone should teach you. But as his anointing teaches you about everything, and is true, and is no lie—just as it has taught you, abide in him." 1 John 2:27

When we consider wisdom coming only and ultimately from the Lord, it reorients our perspective as we seek to grow and mature as believers. Instead of receiving teaching in self-focused fear, either because we are starry-eyed about the speaker or listening to benefit ourselves, we aim to receive teaching with God-focused fear. In the latter posture, we are concerned most about knowing and applying the truth, which can be taught and understood only through God Himself. Think of watershed moments in Christian history. Man did not teach Peter to preach to the Gentiles that they too might be saved (Acts 10). This truth came from God (Acts 10:28). It is confirmed throughout Scripture that salvation is by faith alone and available to anyone, but the revelation came to Peter by the Spirit. Because Peter listened and obeyed, it changed the trajectory of Christianity.

Similarly, Luther was not joined by many people when he posted his theses that reformed the church. Why had centuries of church leaders not confirmed what he came to know as truth? Instead of dismissing it because there was no precedent, God's Word compelled him, and the Spirit convicted him to send forth the truth. God does the same sovereign work for all His people to whom He reveals wonderful things. God sovereignly reveals His ways and plans to those with ears to hear and eyes to see.

These instances do not give license to speak new "truth," as some might claim they have new insight from God that no one else has. False teachers will try to speak new ideas that are not grounded in Scripture, but no new knowledge and understanding exists that Scripture cannot confirm. If someone speaks some revolutionary truth, our first stop should be the canon of Scripture. Where does God's Word substantiate this idea or principle? Next, we can look at those who ran the race and finished well. Did they have thoughts on this idea or principle that Scripture confirms? In some cases, as with Luther and Peter, there may not be such people; but if it is truth, it will stand firm through testing and testing by the Word of God. The Spirit is our wisdom, and He can guide us into all truth (John 16:13). We must yield our minds to His teaching and our bodies to His service.

Active Discernment

> "Everyone then who hears these words of mine and does them will be like a wise man who built his house on the rock… And everyone who hears these words of mine and does not do them will be like a foolish man who built his house on the sand."
> Matthew 7:24, 26

Thoughts and ideas not grounded in truth are merely opinions, and we cannot base our lives on them; therefore, discernment is necessary. We can spend years building our lives on the sands of opinions, thinking we are firmly grounded on the rock, only to find out we were living by our own wisdom the whole time. Jesus closes His Sermon on the Mount with a hopeful promise and sobering warning. He promises that everyone who hears His words and does them will be like a wise man who built his house on the rock but everyone who hears His words and does not do them will be like a foolish man who built his house on the sand.

Jesus tells us to hear His words and do them—not man's words, but God's. We know those words through Scripture and the Spirit. But it doesn't stop there. Wisdom is not simply knowledge but the right knowledge and the right application of that knowledge for the glory of God. It is active. It is holy action. Once we differentiate between right and wrong, our actions confirm whether or not we have spiritual understanding. Knowing this gives weight to even the small things we think and believe in life. If we have unbiblical views and orient our lives around those faulty beliefs, they will lead us the wrong way because we will act according to what we believe. If we believe wrongly, we will act wrongly and busy ourselves in vain. Thus, we are to "destroy arguments and every lofty opinion raised against the knowledge of God, and take every thought captive to obey Christ" (2 Corinthians 10:5). Our actions begin in our minds. If we have the mind of Christ, we have the wisdom and power to discern and do right.

Through Christ in us, as we are taught in Scripture, we can discern right from wrong, as we engage the culture and live with one another. Absolute truth keeps us from veering off the right path. Consider an explorer using his compass to lead him in the right direction. If he is off by even one degree in his calculations, that error will be monumental the longer he continues in the "almost right" direction. We cannot afford to be almost right. Discernment is a necessary part of wisdom as it guides us in the right, not almost right, way.

The Danger of Almost Right

> "Discernment is not knowing the difference between right and wrong. It is knowing the difference between right and almost right." Charles Spurgeon[37]

Every summer, we usually meet my parents for a week of vacation in the same city. They make the long drive from Canada to meet us, saving us the stress of a long road trip with kids. One year we were meeting them at a new condo for the week. Serving as navigator, I dutifully put the address in my phone while my husband started the drive. As we neared our destination, we noticed signs for the city, but our navigation was leading us away from our usual area. "It's a new place," I told Aaron. "Let's just drive a bit more." After 45 minutes of driving farther than we normally do, I called my dad, who confirmed we were not in the right place. I looked back over the directions to ensure the address I typed wasn't leading us to some far-off city. All seemed correct, but then he asked me if I added the "e" to the words "Old" and "Town" in the street name. "What difference does that make?" I thought to myself as I recalled only typing the usual spelling of both words. Technology today is brilliant; it would correct me. But it didn't correct me. It thought I wanted to go to Old Town Road as I requested instead of Olde Towne Road, where I intended. My tiny omissions led our family to the wrong place. To this day, my husband is wary of my navigation on road trips. Whenever we think we are heading in the wrong direction, we give each other this knowing stare.

The address I typed in that summer was almost right, but the almost-right address led us to the wrong place. Spurgeon makes this same crucial

---

[37] Source Unknown.

distinction by separating almost right from right; almost right is not right. Why is this so important? Because if we do not listen to, receive, and apply truth in our lives, we will go the wrong way. We can intend to do the right thing and be doing the wrong thing. We must examine, or test, everything to make sure it is right.

Test Everything

> "Test everything, hold fast to what is good." 1 Thessalonians 5:21

Within the command to fear God, there may be no greater command for our time than the command to test everything. The world has no shortage of false prophets (1 John 4:1) and we can only know they are false by knowing the truth. We need to evaluate every teaching in light of God's Word. To receive any teaching as truth, no matter the platform or fame of the teacher, without testing it against truth is too costly. Some may end up building their lives on mere opinions.

Paul tells us in Romans 12:2, "Do not be conformed to this world but be transformed by the renewal of your mind, that by testing you may discern what is the will of God, what is good and acceptable and perfect." Studying Scripture renews our minds, transforming us. Included in renewing our minds is the ability to discern God's will. The reference to discerning God's will implies action and application because of our transformation. We can also look to the previous verse speaking of presenting our bodies as living sacrifices, holy and acceptable to God.

Those who are wise in their own eyes don't see the need to test everything. Their confidence in their own limited knowledge keeps them from inclining their ear to wisdom. Proverbs 3:7 contrasts the fear of the LORD with being wise in our own eyes. "Be not wise in your own eyes; fear the LORD, and turn away from evil." How do we prove we are not wise in our own eyes? By fearing the LORD and turning away from evil. The two go together. The ultimate purpose of discernment is to know the truth so that we can do what pleases God (Ephesians 5:10). We must rely on the Spirit to help us know and do what is right; this is the high goal of discernment.

1 Thessalonians 5:21 doesn't only tell us to test everything but gives the equally crucial command to "hold fast to what is good." Why test everything

if, when you find the right answer, you don't hold on to it, no matter the cost? As we learned, good is objective. There is a right answer. Unless we hold on to what is good, we will most definitely lose our way. The writer of Hebrews warned about this repeatedly. Holding fast to the truth will save us (Hebrews 3:14). We must trust the truth. "Some trust in chariots and some in horses, but we trust in the name of the LORD our God" (Psalm 20:7). He alone is good, and to Him, we must hold fast even, especially in testing.

Test Me, O God

> "Search me, O God, and know my heart! Try me and know my thoughts! And see if there be any grievous way in me, and lead me in the way everlasting!" Psalm 139:23-24

As we test everything, God is testing us too (Exodus 20:20, James 1:3). Just as our testing is to discern what is good and evil so we can hold fast to what is good, God tests us to root out our grievous (evil) ways and lead us in the (good) way everlasting. God tests us so that the fear of God may be before us that we may not sin (Exodus 20:20). Before Him, the state of our hearts is what matters most of all; so we ask God to search our hearts, reveal our sins through testing and trials, and lead us in the right(eous) way. If anyone knows the condition of our hearts, it is God; and He can help us see what He sees.

CHAPTER 15

Self-Awareness

"The heart is deceitful above all things, and desperately sick; who can understand it?" Jeremiah 17:9

"Nearly all the wisdom which we possess, that is to say, true and sound wisdom, consists of two parts: the knowledge of God and of ourselves." John Calvin[38]

Christianity is not for good people. There are no good people. In our flesh, we are capable of any sin, and we all fall short of the glory of God (Romans 3:23). The Spirit convicts us of our sins and areas of greatest weakness, reminding us that apart from Christ, we can do nothing good (John 15:5). Because the kingdom of God is full of flips and reversals, those who know and confess they are inadequate, ill-equipped, and fall short in every way of God's perfect expectation are the ones He welcomes and uses for His glory. Henry Allen Ironside reminds us, "God is looking for broken men who have judged themselves in the light of the cross of Christ. When He wants anything done, He takes up men who have come to the end of themselves, whose confidence is not in themselves, but in God."[39]

The Foolish and the Wise

> "But God chose what is foolish in the world to shame the wise; God chose what is weak in the world to shame the strong; God

---

[38] Calvin, John. 2008. *Institutes of the Christian Religion.* Hendrickson Publishers, Revised Edition.

[39] Letellier, Shauna. 2017. *Remarkable Faith: When Jesus Marveled at the Faith of Unremarkable People.* FaithWords.

chose what is low and despised in the world, even things that are not, to bring to nothing things that are, so that no human being might boast in the presence of God. And because of him you are in Christ Jesus, who became to us wisdom from God, righteousness and sanctification and redemption, so that, as it is written, 'Let the one who boasts, boast in the Lord.'"
1 Corinthians 1:27-31

Those who know Christ have the wisdom and power of God. The magnificence and majesty of this reality are shocking. From the world's perspective, it is also shocking that God entrusted the foolish with this wisdom and power. In revealing His wisdom to the meek and lowly, He shames the proud who feel entitled to the wisdom and power. This is evident in the gospels as we see the juxtaposition of the disciples and the Jewish leaders. Those who followed Jesus, His closest twelve disciples, and other men and women were mostly uneducated. After Pentecost, God's very power and wisdom through the Holy Spirit filled them. As they proclaimed Christ crucified, the Church grew. Many new believers were not men and women of noble stature in the religious communities. They were foolish, lesser people in the eyes of those who cared about status.

On the other hand, the religious leaders were wise in their own eyes. They knew the laws, they lived externally "good" lives, and they valued their own wisdom. As with other paradigms in the Bible, it was not the latter who received wisdom from God but the former—the ones who did not think much of themselves or their knowledge, status, or power.

Humility and Self-Awareness

"We have no works in which we can glory; for even if we have an abundance of good works, they are all God's works in us, and we give Him all the praise for them." Charles Spurgeon[40]

Humility is a precious virtue that can be easily misunderstood. While humility is identifiable, it is not always in the ways we might think. Those who downplay the good things they do or try to stay out of the spotlight may be considered humble. But humility is more profound; it's not just external gestures. It starts inside and works its way out. It is a state of heart that will

---

[40] Spurgeon, Charles. 1901. *The Metropolitan Tabernacle Pulpit Sermons, Volume 47.* Passmore & Alabaster.

not always look quiet and private. Jesus was humble yet bold and performed miracles witnessed by few and many. Paul, who called himself the worst of sinners, told people to imitate him (1 Corinthians 4:16, 11:1). As we read his letters, we notice a very different kind of humility than the type we might think of in our churches today. If we heard people saying, "imitate me," we would label them as some of the most arrogant people in the church. Yet Paul was a godly example for us. How do we reconcile that?

How could Paul be humble and yet tell others to imitate him? C.S. Lewis says the humble person "will not be thinking about humility: he will not be thinking about himself at all."[41] Paul was not thinking of himself when calling on others to imitate him because he thought much of God. He knew it was the power of Christ doing all his good works. To bring glory to God, he lived in submission to Him. By telling others to look at his life, he was not saying, "Look at me!" He was saying, "Look at the glory of God displayed in me by the power of Christ. Look at what a gracious, loving, and merciful God can do with such a sinner as me." He did not draw attention to himself; he drew attention to God in his life. The Spirit of God at work in us compels other believers to pursue Him. Paul was a visual example of what God could do in and through His people and an example of the humility the Church needs today.

Letting Your Light Shine

> "'You are the light of the world. A city set on a hill cannot be hidden. Nor do people light a lamp and put it under a basket, but on a stand, and it gives light to all in the house. In the same way, let your light shine before others, so that they may see your good works and give glory to your Father who is in heaven.'"
> Matthew 5:14-16

"Visible humility" is so contrary to "hidden humility" that we often consider to be the right way. The visibility of our works can easily lead to pride as we get attention and admiration from others; but a humble heart recognizes that no good work is done by us. Yes, telling others to imitate us as Paul did can be risky.

Paul and Barnabas give a helpful picture of a humble response to worldly praise. We need this instruction if we are going to shine in a world that adores

---

[41] Lewis, C. S. 2001. *Mere Christianity*. HarperOne.

idols. On Paul and Barnabas's missionary journey to Lystra, Paul commanded a crippled man to stand up. He saw this man listening intently to him and discerned that he had faith to be made well. By the power of God, the man sprang up and began walking (Acts 14:10). The crowds saw what happened and they were amazed. They could not associate that power with anyone except the gods they worshiped. They thought Paul and Barnabas were their gods, Zeus and Hermes, working these great miracles (Acts 14:11-12). The people wanted to worship them as their idols; when Paul and Barnabas heard this, they tore their clothes and rushed out of the crowd. They felt shame because they could not imagine taking credit for what God alone did. They took that opportunity to turn the eyes of the people from worldly idols to Jesus Christ as they gave Him all the praise and glory.

We all struggle with idol worship, even in our churches. These idols are often worldly comforts; sometimes they are pastors or ministry leaders, but most of the time, the idol we worship is ourselves. We are impressed with ourselves. We think much of ourselves. We want to please ourselves. We give the most consideration and weight to our own thoughts and opinions. While God alone is worthy of all our love and adoration, we give it to ourselves. Instead of living empowered by God-focused fear, we live in self-focused fear. Foolishly, we worship the created instead of the Creator. Why? Because we have distorted the truth about ourselves and the truth about God. Rather than believing God is the giver of all things, including our gifts and abilities, we blind ourselves to that truth and try to take credit for things we could not do without Him. Balancing a right view of ourselves with a right view of God can keep us from pride's toxicity, which will steal God's glory every time. In humility, it's right to experience a sense of shame when people try to attribute God's work to us, but that shame should turn our hearts and theirs to the glory of God.

The Westminster Catechism says the chief end of man is to glorify God and enjoy Him forever. If we believe that is true, we will not downplay or avoid opportunities He ordains to display His work in our lives. "For we are His workmanship, created in Christ Jesus for good works, which God prepared beforehand, that we should walk in them" (Ephesians 2:10). Through His sanctifying work in our lives, we can show the world with our lives just how great our God is. His glory knows no bounds. He can change a sinner like me, and thus, he can change a sinner like you! The world hungers for this glorious hope.

Understanding Ourselves

> "They that know God will be humble. They that know themselves cannot be proud." John Flavel[42]

Christians are to live as changed people, but we are also changing people. God's sanctifying work is lifelong as we continuously battle the flesh. Our hearts can still deceive us. We say we don't want power, glory, or attention, but our sinful longings are for those very things. We can convince ourselves that our true feelings are not true, but God knows our hearts. He knows our deepest desires and the sins we struggle to rid ourselves of in our own power. So, as we seek to understand God and His Word, as we ask Him to give us wisdom in various situations, we should also ask Him to give us an understanding of ourselves. We should study ourselves as vulnerably and transparently as we study God and His Word. We do this not to condemn ourselves, but so the Spirit can convict our hearts and turn us from our sins.

When we think of God and praise Him for His majesty and glory, we should remember who we were and who we would be apart from Christ. We can also consider who we are when we act apart from Him. To do this practically, we can ask ourselves questions like: Where are my weaknesses in the flesh? Where do I need the strength of God that I have been neglecting? What are my sinful tendencies? My secret sins? This self-awareness should place us rightly at the foot of the cross and not lead us to despair. We are broken sinners at the cross with grateful hearts worshiping God for His gracious gift of salvation by faith in Jesus Christ. We certainly don't deserve it.

When we ask the Spirit to show us our sins and weaknesses, we are asking Him to shine light where it is dark. In this practice of self-study, the Spirit will shine light in the dark places of our lives—the places that we didn't even know were dark. In the dark, our sins fester and go unnoticed (but not unnoticed by God). If we ignore or deny them, how can we turn from them? But when they are brought to light by His loving-kindness, this self-awareness can lead us, as broken sinners, to repentance. This practice is invaluable as it brings glory to God by turning us from self-focused fears (sins) to God-focused fear (holiness). We need simply to ask Him to light the way and help us walk in it.

---

[42] Flavel, John. 2013. *The Method of Grace*. Bottom of the Hill Publishing.

CHAPTER 16

Prayer

"Rejoice always, pray without ceasing, give thanks in all circumstances; for this is the will of God in Christ Jesus for you." 1 Thessalonians 5:16-18

"Pray often; for prayer is a shield to the soul, a sacrifice to God, and a scourge for Satan." John Bunyan[43]

We have confined prayer to such a small and specific box. In our own wisdom, we can't see outside this man-made perception of prayer to understand just how big the box is supposed to be. With self-awareness comes a glaring recognition that we need a Savior, not only at the start of our faith journey, but every moment of that journey. The wise know they need help to please God, help that is beyond their own effort. There is a necessary dependence that characterizes the wise. When we filter prayer down to its primary element, it is just that: dependence on God. The wise person depends on God, so the wise person prays.

Growing up in church, I generally defined prayer as me talking to God. Even as a young adult attending prayer meetings, praying corporately with the church, or praying alone, I found myself limiting prayer to a formal interaction with God. I thought prayer was different than the rest of my day. It was the time when I was really talking to God. It was sacred and special. That's why people talk about how important it is: "We need to be people of prayer!" We believe prayer is the most powerful thing we can do, so it's first on the list when we endeavor to do something. But what if prayer is not the first thing on the list? What if prayer is the list?

---

[43] Bunyan, John. 2015. *Delphi Complete Works of John Bunyan* (Illustrated). Delphi Classics.

Abiding and Prayer

> "Abide in me, and I in you. As the branch cannot bear fruit by itself, unless it abides in the vine, neither can you, unless you abide in me. I am the vine; you are the branches. Whoever abides in me and I in him, he it is that bears much fruit, for apart from me you can do nothing." John 15:4-5

Jesus illustrates our union with Himself in many ways throughout the gospels. In John 15, He calls us to abide in Him; He uses a vine and its branches to illustrate how it looks to abide in Jesus Christ. It's a helpful visual when we apply it to our relationship with Jesus. A branch is only healthy and living when connected to the vine. The vine is the branch's life source. As the branch remains connected to the vine, it produces the fruit associated with it. If it is a healthy branch, it will produce much fruit; but it will also require pruning so that it can produce even more fruit. Without the vine, the branch cannot bear fruit and, it dies. Scripture often uses the phrase "in Christ" to communicate the same truth; our life necessarily connects to Jesus Christ and our intimacy with Him. If we are not in Christ, we are not abiding in Him and cannot bear fruit. Jesus plainly says we can do nothing apart from Him (John 15:5).

What does abiding and being in Christ have to do with prayer? Looking at prayer only as a formal conversation with God, as we sometimes do in the church, we often think of ourselves as separate from God when we pray. Scripture is clear that when we are in Christ, we are in fellowship with God, in communion with Him—this abiding relationship is made possible by the blood of Jesus shed on the cross. When we believe in Jesus Christ's redeeming work to save us, we are "in Christ." It is who we are. We become tethered to Him, not separate from Him. Our life comes from His life. Our fruit is His fruit. We are just the branch, the channel through which He can manifest His life to the world. We are to always abide in Him. At no point is it wise to pull ourselves away from Him, but sometimes we do when we pray. We think of ourselves as separate from Him, but in this most intimate time of communion with God, we should be abiding in Him because apart from Christ, we have no righteousness of our own to be able to approach Him. Jesus Christ is the means through which we can approach God's throne of grace dependent on Him for all things, our needs, and life itself.

Petitioning and Prayer

> "If you abide in me, and my words abide in you, ask whatever you wish, and it will be done for you. By this my Father is glorified, that you bear much fruit and so prove to be my disciples." John 15:7-8

In this passage about abiding, Jesus addresses one aspect of prayer we are very familiar with: petitioning. There are similar verses throughout Scripture (John 14:13, 1 John 3:22, 1 John 5:14). Some see these verses as a freedom to ask for whatever and believe that God will give it to them. While Jesus does make it open-ended, it is still conditional. The latter is only true with the former. We must abide in Christ, and His Word must abide in us. When His words abide in us, they are His words we speak, and it is His will we seek. "Delight yourself in the LORD and He will give you the desires of your heart" (Psalm 37:4). When we delight in the LORD, the desires of our hearts are first His desires that He put in our hearts. He takes great pleasure in giving them to us as they were His desires first, and He put them there to bring glory to Himself.

Confidence in having our petitions answered comes not from faith in and of itself but from the Source of our faith. It is not the act of prayer that brings power or effects change; it is the Source of our prayer. Another important factor as we abide in Christ is: Who is praying? There are only two options. Either we pray in the flesh, in self-focused fear, or we pray in the Spirit, with God-focused fear. The former does not please God and the latter does please Him (Romans 8:5-8).

James comments on our petitions—the right ones we don't ask for and the wrong ones we do. He says, "You do not have, because you do not ask. You ask and do not receive, because you ask wrongly, to spend it on your passions" (James 4:2-3). The passions we want to spend our fleshly requests on are self-focused. We ask for these when we are not abiding in Jesus. They do not please God because they are not what God wants for us.

God wants to give us all things in Christ, but we do not have many of those things because we don't ask for them. We don't think we need them while we live in our own wisdom and power. Earlier in James's letter, he calls those who lack wisdom to ask God for it, and He will give it generously (James 1:5). This is wisdom from the Holy Spirit that helps us understand and apply what God wants to teach us. We cannot pray in a way that pleases God without the Spirit because we cannot commune with God without the Spirit. Prayer is not merely man talking to God, but the Spirit in man communing with God and joining Him in His good desires for us.

Pray without Ceasing

> "Likewise the Spirit helps us in our weakness. For we do not know what to pray for as we ought, but the Spirit himself intercedes for us with groanings too deep for words. And he who searches hearts knows what is the mind of the Spirit, because the Spirit intercedes for the saints according to the will of God." Romans 8:26-27

Paul addresses the times we don't ask for the right things and ask for the wrong things. He tells us in his letter to the Romans that even when we are weak in the flesh and don't pray as we ought, the Spirit is still working to accomplish God's good plans for us. We are needy people, but we are often confused about what we truly need or don't realize just how needy we are. In those times of self-focused passions or pride, we are not abiding, but the Spirit is still working.

1 Thessalonians 5:17 helps us understand God's command that we pray without ceasing. The command seems impossible, especially when we think about the number of times we do not depend on Jesus Christ for life and godliness. For man, it is impossible, but with God, all things are possible; He does not command us to do something He cannot equip us to do. Those in Christ have the indwelling Holy Spirit who intercedes for us according to God's sovereign will. The command to pray without ceasing is possible when we see prayer as an all-encompassing communion with God instead of only a specific time when we fold our hands and close our eyes. Prayer is not isolated moments of praise and petition but a constant calling on Jesus—a constant yielding to and abiding in Him. The Spirit helps us do that.

The Holy Spirit helps us commune with God and produce the good fruit of that communion which is possible through our abiding relationship with Jesus Christ. In our flesh, we fail to abide perfectly; but the Spirit continues to advocate before the Father for us. In our flesh, we lack the wisdom to ask for the right things and not ask for the wrong things. Without the help of the Spirit, we cannot pray according to God's sovereign will because we do not know it, thus the importance of God's Word abiding in us. We know the *will* of God through the *Word* of God by the *Spirit* of God. When we *know* the Word of God, we can *pray* for the will of God *by* the Spirit of God. Prayer in the Spirit accomplishes God's purposes for His glory. When we broaden our view of prayer, we begin to understand how this command is not only possible but accomplished. John Bunyan described prayer well when he said prayer "is the opener of the heart of God, and a means by which the soul, though empty, is filled."[44] When we pray without ceasing, the heart of God fills our souls. The Spirit fills us, equipping us with His wisdom to ask and think and say and do as He leads.

Wisdom on Full Display

> "If you keep my commandments, you will abide in my love, just as I have kept my Father's commandments and abide in his love. These things I have spoken to you, that my joy may be in you, and that your joy may be full." John 15:10-11

Prayer is the Christian's greatest display of wisdom. We know just how foolish we are, how weak and needy, and how sinful and lifeless we are apart from Christ. We also know we cannot obey Him apart from His help. With that understanding, we go to Him—not just once a week, not just once a day—but as often as we see our need. Interestingly, a Christian's awareness of his or her need doesn't decrease with time. It increases. Those growing in wisdom and the fear of the LORD don't become more independent from Christ but more dependent on Christ. The more we depend on Him, the more we will abide in Him. Through prayerful dependence on Jesus Christ for all things, He provides for every need, the ones we know and those we don't. He delights in providing for us. As we enjoy the sweetness of abiding in Him as we obey Him, He gives us fullness of joy. Whether in the painful pruning seasons or the exciting time of harvest, we can rejoice in knowing the vinedresser, in His perfect wisdom, is caring for us well as we abide in the true vine. He is love, after all.

---

[44] Bunyan, John. 2012. *The Works of John Bunyan: Experimental, Doctrinal, and Practical.* Nabu Press.

PART IV

Love and the Fear of God

CHAPTER 17

Love and Fear

"God is love, and whoever abides in love abides in God, and God abides in him. By this is love perfected with us, so that we may have confidence for the day of judgment, because as he is so also are we in this world. There is no fear in love, but perfect love casts out fear. For fear has to do with punishment, and whoever fears has not been perfected in love. We love because he first loved us."
1 John 4:16-19

"Love through me, love of God; there is no love in me. O Fire of love, light Thou the love that burns perpetually." Amy Carmichael[45]

Every Mother's Day, my daughter proudly presents me with a couple of special creations. One year she gave me a cute card that stated on the front, "I Hope Your Mother's Day is Berry Sweet!" Inside the berry-themed card was a short rhyme that ended with a list of reasons why she loves me: "She gives me hugs, she reads me stories, she loves me." As I frequently reread the card displayed on our mantle that month, I thought of 1 John 4:19 and what a Christian's list might look like if we named all the reasons why we love God. There could be a million reasons but only one really matters: We love God because He first loved us. That one statement sums up the entire gospel. His love for us, demonstrated by sending Jesus to die on the cross for our sins so we might have a restored relationship with Him, enables our response of love for Him. Without God's love for us, we could not love Him in return. My sweet daughter loves me because I love her, but nothing compares to God's love for His children, and our only response to that steadfast love is to love Him.

---

[45] Carmichael, Amy. 1988. *Toward Jerusalem*. CLC Publications.

Love and God-Focused Fear

One of the greatest identifying marks of those who fear God is their love for God and others. Loving God and fearing Him are inseparable—those who love God fear Him, and those who fear God love Him. John tells us in 1 John 4 that God is love and those who abide in love abide in God, and He abides in them; this clarifies the necessity of God's involvement in our love. He empowers and cultivates it as we abide, or remain tethered to Him, like a branch to its vine. As we abide in Him, love and God-focused fear are perfected in us.

Love and Self-Focused Fear

> "There is no fear in love, but perfect love casts out fear. For fear has to do with punishment, and whoever fears has not been perfected in love." 1 John 4:18

Understanding the difference between God-focused and self-focused fear helps clarify what Scripture says in verse 18. John explains that "there is no fear in love, but perfect love casts out fear." Here we see the negative, self-focused fear, also known as servile fear, that we considered earlier. We know this because John says, "fear has to do with punishment, and whoever fears has not been perfected in love." We were not made to love God with this kind of fear as Romans 8:15 and Luke 1:74 confirm. Love, who is God Himself, cannot co-exist with self-focused fear; but perfect love, who is God Himself, casts out self-focused fear. Psalm 34:4 and Exodus 20:20 both describe how the fear of the Lord drives out any other fears. Love drives self-focused fear out.

Perfect love casts out self-focused fear because perfect love is God Himself. Self-focused fear flees in His presence. The hope-filled promise is that when we abide in God, His love abides in us and His presence casts out our self-focused fear. In his letter to Timothy, Paul encouraged him with similar words reminding us that "God gave us a spirit not of fear but of power and love and self-control" (2 Timothy 1:7). The Holy Spirit is with us to overcome self-focused fear. In Him, we have God's power and love and the fruit of self-control to fight against our flesh. As we rely on the Spirit for these things and He works them in our lives, we demonstrate our love for (and fear of) God.

Love for One Another

> "By this all people will know that you are my disciples, if you have love for one another." John 13:35

Love that proves we fear God will always be God-focused, for His glory and to please Him. But it will also extend to those around us. If we love God, we will love others. When rooted in the fear of God, our love for others will look like Christ's love, which will be the love of God Himself in us. The measureless love we receive from Him enables us to show that same love to others.

The world has all sorts of ideas about love and what it looks like but Christians love as God calls and empowers us to love. This doesn't mean we always love rightly; but when we are led by the Spirit, we will love rightly. However, the reality is that self-focused fear easily creeps into our love. It happens when we yield to our flesh when we "love." It can happen when we try to serve others but do so for our benefit or praise. It can also happen when we are called to love in hard ways; we become more concerned about ourselves and the repercussions of doing the hard but loving thing.

If Christians love as Christ loves, we must know this is not always and only a gentle and meek love. It is sometimes a strong, firm, and sacrificial love. It will call us to deny ourselves for the glory of God and the benefit of others. It may call us to be silent and not revile those who revile against us; but at other times, it may call us to speak the truth. If silence in love spares others from greater sin, that may be what the Spirit commands for a time; but other times, the Spirit may command we speak to confront sin, that it might cease, with love as our driving force. When the Spirit leads us to remain silent in love or speak in love, these can be difficult moments. They are difficult because of our tendency toward self-focused fear. We are often thinking about defending ourselves or we're concerned with how others will react or treat us when we speak the truth. But when God's love fills our hearts, His glory will supersede any of our self-focused fears whether the Spirit leads us to remain silent or to speak.

Love and Truth

> "[Love] does not rejoice at wrongdoing, but rejoices with the truth." 1 Corinthians 13:6

One of the most glaring differences between God's love and the "love" that masquerades in the world as the real thing is the necessary value God's love places on truth. Love that forsakes or denies the truth is not love.

Love will never deny or forfeit the truth. Instead, love will rejoice with the truth no matter what the truth is. I don't mean truth is subjective; it is not. The objectivity of truth has never been under attack more than it is today. Love values the truth and is willing to search for it, find it, and appreciate it, even if the truth is hard. Christians believe hard truths. We know the truth of our sin is a hard truth. We know that apart from Christ we would be dead in our sins, another hard truth. Life is full of hard truths. We don't deny them because they are hard; we receive them because they are true.

The Church sometimes struggles with blurred lines between love and truth. While they should be one, we have tried to divide them. We do this most often when the truth is hard or when truth requires us to do something hard. We think by softening or suppressing truth, we are more loving. Some churches are lessening the harshness of our sin to make more people feel "loved." In doing so, they are not showing love because it sacrifices the hard truth of the depths of our depravity. Jesus came to expose our sin so we would turn from it when confronted with truth and love.

While love rejoices with the truth, love does not rejoice in unrighteousness. In other words, while we receive the truth of our sin, we do not celebrate it. Love does not embrace or affirm sin. When love dwells in us, the Spirit convicts us of our sin. The Spirit shines a light on our sin to expose the truth of it, so that we can be rid of it and grow in righteousness—this is love. If our focus is "love" while forsaking the truth, we are not loving or growing in righteousness. We must speak and receive the truth in love to grow into Christlikeness (Ephesians 4:15).

Love's High Standard

> "Love is patient and kind; love does not envy or boast; it is not arrogant or rude. It does not insist on its own way; it is

not irritable or resentful; it does not rejoice at wrongdoing, but rejoices with the truth. Love bears all things, believes all things, hopes all things, endures all things. Love never ends."
1 Corinthians 13:4-8

Love calls us to an impossibly high standard. A widely referenced passage, 1 Corinthians 13, describes the high standard of love. We have touched on some specifics already, but it's important to note that love is not one of the descriptors in isolation. Love is not simply one of these characteristics but all of them. It includes every listed description. For example, to love patiently but with envy is not love. To defer to another's way resentfully is not love. For us to demonstrate love, we must encompass all things at once.

Also, consider the beginning of verse 8: "Love never ends." This idea of never-ending love brings love to a different dimension because even this world is not forever. In our flesh, and on this earth, never-ending love is an impossibility. How can we love at all? It appears the standard is too high, the requirements too rigorous, and the eternality unattainable. Yet, we are commanded to love, so there must be some way to accomplish it.

This descriptor of eternal love alone is enough for us to confess our need for Jesus Christ to live and love in and through us. We cannot look within ourselves or even within our world to accomplish what only God can do in us. If we believe that God is love, then the commanded love we are to show is not subjective but the objective love of God in Jesus Christ. He is perfect love. While we may break from perfect love, when we sin and cease abiding, we can turn back to Him and continue communing with Him, whose love never ends and who is love that never ends. When we trust in Jesus, turning away from our self-focused fear to live in God-focused fear, He fills us with perfect love that empowers us to love God and others with our entire being. That relationship through Jesus Christ gives us access to God the Father, giving us every spiritual blessing (Ephesians 1:3), including the ability to love.

The love we receive in our hearts when we are born again is the inward love that enables us to demonstrate external love; this love displays all characteristics at once and never ends. We do not love perfectly or eternally, but God does. "So we have come to know and to believe the love that God has for us. God is love, and whoever abides in love abides in God, and God abides in him" (1 John 4:16). When we fear God through Jesus, abiding in Him by His Spirit, we can love as God called us to love because He is in us and with us.

CHAPTER 18

The Significance of Love

"If I speak in the tongues of men and of angels, but have not love, I am a noisy gong or a clanging cymbal. And if I have prophetic powers, and understand all mysteries and all knowledge, and if I have all faith, so as to remove mountains, but have not love, I am nothing. If I give away all I have, and if I deliver up my body to be burned, but have not love, I gain nothing." 1 Corinthians 13:1-3

"The most inveterate obstacle in mastering the lesson [of love] is SELF, which persists with an energy which nothing but divine grace can overcome. When no longer we seek our own in any of our relations with others, we have learned to love. Until then, we still need to stay in Christ's school." J. R. Miller[46]

As J. R. Miller states, the greatest hindrance to love is self. As long as we are the focus and purpose of our love, we are not demonstrating love because "love does not seek its own." Knowing when self is the focus and purpose of love can be challenging to identify. But it doesn't take long for us to look around in just about any setting, even churches, and see the damaging effect of self-focused fear. We are dealing with two problems: a lack of love and an abundance of misdirected "love." Instead of love established in the fear of God for His glory and the benefit of others, we see "love" based in self for the glory and benefit of ourselves.

The previous chapter briefly examined love as God defines it in 1 Corinthians 13. Too often, though, we head straight to that description of love, skipping Paul's emphatic warning of acting apart from love (1 Cor 13:1-3). His warning cautions us to carefully consider the words we speak and

---

[46] Miller, J. R. 1910. *Learning to Love*. New York, T. Y. Crowell and Co.

the things we do. Even when we act in ways that man's eye may praise, God knows if those acts are rooted in right love (God-focused fear) or wrong love (self-focused fear). Paul's warning allows us to evaluate our lives, considering if and how we are acting in love or apart from it. As he makes clear, it can be hard to tell from the outside. Paul describes each case in which our speech, actions, or religious behavior may look externally good but warns that even these can be in vain if they are done apart from love.

Distracting Speech

> "If I speak in the tongues of men and of angels, but have not love,
> I am a noisy gong or clanging cymbal." 1 Corinthians 13:1

Paul's first warning focuses on our speech declaring the language of men or angels without a heart of love to be nothing more than irritating distractions. Paul's illustration of the noisy gong or clanging cymbal is effective. Imagine an orchestra playing together harmoniously. Each instrument follows the conductor's lead as they play their unique sounds, creating beautiful music. Suddenly, the cymbals start clanging spontaneously and with much gusto without being cued. Their desire to draw attention to themselves was successful but distracting. Though they may have special parts to play at just the right time and the right dynamic, the cymbals felt those instructions denied them the opportunity to showcase their talent. They wanted a moment of their own to show what they could do. In doing so, however, they ruined the experience for patrons attending what was supposed to be an event with beautiful music. And so it should be with us: the purpose of our speech should not be to showcase ourselves, but to glorify God through the loving words that are in accordance with His instruction and direction. Too often, we selfishly position ourselves to be heard and known, like the cymbals. If the reasons for our words are to receive praise and glory for ourselves, we are self-focused, not loving, but distracting from the One who is love.

Social Media, Tongues of Men, and Noisy Gongs

Social media has made it possible to make any statements, opinions, and thoughts we have public. Thoughts that would typically only be known to us and those nearest us are now available to the world. While these platforms could allow for more loving speech in our world, they have instead set the stage for more opportunities to bang our noisy gongs. Before, we could privately praise a friend, encourage a spouse, exhort a child, or compliment a co-worker. Out of the overflow of our hearts, we would speak and there wouldn't be hundreds (thousands, or millions) of listeners. Now, social media has changed how we interact with each other.

Our concern and focus, by default and sinful nature, is on ourselves. Even the sweetest encouragement to a friend on their birthday can become distorted if we spend time crafting our message so that others will be impressed with our kindness and eloquence. Like the noisy gong, social media has given us a stage to be seen and heard in ways that were never possible. They have created room for more sin rather than less. So, we are left to evaluate the motive behind why we post what we post, which can lead us more broadly to evaluate why we say what we say, both privately and publicly.

Teaching, Tongues of Angels, and Clanging Cymbals

> "No amount of scholastic attainment, of able and profound exposition of brilliant and stirring eloquence can atone for the absence of a deep impassioned sympathetic love for human souls." David Brainerd[47]

Paul warned that even those who speak in the tongues of angels could do so apart from love. This warning is timely, as we battle for truth and hear contradicting messages daily. If anyone speaks of God and His Word apart from the motivation of love for Him and others, it's nothing but clanging cymbals. Love for God and others must motivate everything we do, say, and think. The church can miss this crucial point regarding our speech. Sometimes we assume that because we are Christians, we are free to say whatever we want, but we can speak without love whenever we speak according to our flesh and not the Spirit; this is an especially weighty point for teachers. We make every effort to be instructive, have good illustrations, demonstrate a commitment to the text, and be theologically sound; and yet, if the love of God does not drive our hearts, our speech can distract people from God instead of pointing them

---

[47] Brainerd, David, and Jonathan Edwards. 2019. *The Life and Diary of David Brainerd.* Benediction Classics.

to Him. If love does not compel us to say what we say, then our "holy" words can be clanging distractions doing more damage than good.

The Worthlessness of Religiosity

> "And if I have prophetic powers, and understand all mysteries and all knowledge, and if I have all faith, so as to remove mountains, but have not love, I am nothing." 1 Corinthians 13:2

Besides our speech, Paul addresses our religiosity without love. The ability to prophecy, understand and explain complexities of the Bible, or even have tremendous faith do not alone prove our relationship with God. The love of Christ Himself must drive them. Paul says without love propelling these abilities, "we are nothing." Paul's warning is appropriate as we can be so impressed with ourselves when we articulate a spiritual truth eloquently or receive a most incredible answer to a faith-filled prayer we boldly petitioned. In our flesh, we want to take credit for these great works, but we cannot. If done without love, these acts or abilities don't qualify us; they nullify us. We can claim no credit for any good thing. "'For who has known the mind of the Lord, or who has been his counselor?' 'Or who has given a gift to him that he might be repaid?' For from him and through him and to him are all things. To him be glory forever. Amen" (Romans 11:34-36).

The Pharisees were experts in the Law. For many of these religious leaders, the Law was distorted into religiosity when it was given as a teacher and revealer of God Himself. Instead of seeing love in the Word of God, they saw rules to try to obey on their own. They found their identity in their perceived ability to fulfill the Law; but they failed in striving to fulfill the Law without love. Their works were nothing but filthy rags before God (Isaiah 64:6) as are our religious acts apart from God's empowering by His Spirit.

Selflessness Without Love: Selfishness

> "If I give away all I have, and if I deliver up my body to be burned, but have not love, I gain nothing." 1 Corinthians 1:3

We can do anything with selfish motives, even selfless-looking things. For this reason, Paul warns us to check our "selflessness." Giving away all we own and even giving our bodies up in death may seem like the most selfless things we could do, but they could be for our own praise and recognition. If these sacrificial acts are not because of love, we gain nothing from them. Paradoxically, selflessness without love is selfishness. Love puts all the attention on God and others, so the absence of love leaves attention on ourselves.

We fall short of God's command to love others well because we are doing it selfishly, and sometimes, we wrongly follow the world's ever-changing edicts on what love is and how it looks. If we give in to man's demands on what selfless love looks like instead of looking at the perfect example in Christ, we will fail to be selfless every time. Why? Because we are looking to man to define what selflessness is. God defines and accomplishes selflessness in His people through His love manifested in our lives in the person of Jesus Christ. Jesus perfectly demonstrated what it means to consider others better than ourselves and what it means to lay one's life down for a friend. We must rely on Christ and His love to truly live selflessly. Any "selfless" act we do is not truly selfless unless it is Christ in us, loving through us.

The Love of Christ

> "For the love of Christ controls us, because we have concluded this: that one has died for all, therefore all have died; and he died for all, that those who live might no longer live for themselves but for him who for their sake died and was raised."
> 2 Corinthians 5:14-15

Love is first invisible before it becomes visible. Its source and power are Christ in us. Love that is overflowing from the heart. Love that is not for ourselves, not in self-focused fear, but for the LORD and His glory. Paul's warning in these first three verses ultimately drives us to examine our hearts to determine what kind of love drives all we do. Is it love for ourselves or love found in Christ? What is it that controls us?

CHAPTER 19

A Heart that Fears

*"Teach me your way, O LORD, that I may walk in your truth;
unite my heart to fear your name." Psalm 86:11*

*"If Christ is not all to you, He is nothing to you. He will never go into
partnership as a part Savior of men. If He be something He must be everything,
and if He be not everything, He is nothing to you." Charles Spurgeon*[48]

Our hearts are battlegrounds. Every day we are in a spiritual war between good and evil, right and wrong, righteousness and sin, and God-focused and self-focused fears. Ultimately, it is a daily battle between the flesh and the Spirit. Will we love and submit to our flesh or will we love and submit to the Spirit? Too often, we try to live in the land of "both, and." We try to honor God while also clinging to worldly affections. We try to do everything on our to-do list and on God's to-do list, constantly finding our time divided among many good and bad things. I can attest to some of these challenges as a stay-at-home mom with kids who are still quite dependent, a husband serving in vocational ministry, and several personal responsibilities. My heart is too often divided.

Proverbs says, "Keep your heart with all vigilance, for from it flow the springs of life" (Proverbs 4:23). We cannot guard just a section of our hearts for God, for godly things, and spiritual disciplines. We are to guard our whole heart that it might be wholly His; in doing so He can work His love into every part of our lives as we live for Him.

---

[48] Spurgeon, Charles H. 2014. *Spurgeon on Christ*. Bridge-Logos Foundation.

David asked the LORD to unite his heart to fear His name. I notice three truths in his prayer from Psalm 86:

- He asked God to do the work. David could not unite his heart himself.
- He asked God to unite his heart, knowing that is the only way to fear God.
- The purpose of the united heart is to fear God.

David asked, knowing that his tendency as a sinful person was toward a divided heart, a heart full of self-focused fears. A heart divided among many affections will fail to love any one thing rightly. God acknowledges this truth many times in Scripture: a house divided cannot stand (Mark 3:25), you cannot serve God and money (Matthew 6:24), you cannot be lukewarm, neither hot nor cold (Revelation 3:16). You cannot love God wholeheartedly while having a divided heart. David knew this, pleading with the LORD to unite his heart. Our hearts can be united in love for the wrong or the right thing; David wanted a united heart to fear His name, which is the only right purpose for a united heart. He recognized it was only possible through God, and he could not make any effort to unite his heart to fear God on his own or in his own power.

The gospel unites our hearts to fear God. Jesus Christ made the only way for us to fear God in His death and resurrection. Apart from the gospel, there is no possible way to fear God because we have no ability within ourselves to love God completely. We are sinful people who constantly divide our affections; sometimes, we even believe we are right to do it. But if our love is not singular and God-focused, it is in vain. The Bible tells us story after story of our failure as humans to love God and devote our hearts to Him completely. The Bible also tells us story after story of God's intervention to help His people do what only He can do: love and fear Him.

The Dangers of a Divided Heart

> "For the eyes of the LORD roam throughout the earth, so that He may strongly support those whose heart is completely His."
> 2 Chronicles 16:9 (NASB)

Upon being made king of Judah, Asa loved God and established many spiritual changes that honored God. He removed idols so the people would worship God alone. He was God-focused, trusting Him and praying to Him. God blessed Asa and delivered him many times, once specifically from the powerful Ethiopian and Libyan armies. Over time, however, his zeal and faithfulness to God faded. His heart began to divide among many things, and God became just one of those things. Over time, the expectation of God's favor superseded his desire to know, love, and obey God with unity of heart.

In his thirty-sixth year reigning as king, Asa faced a challenge. Instead of turning to God as he did at first, with single-hearted devotion, his heart sought another way out, trusting in his own means and connections. A seer, Hanani, reminded King Asa of how God faithfully delivered his people from the Ethiopians and Libyans because he relied on the LORD. Sadly, Asa's divided heart was not devoted to God, loving and trusting Him as he had before. After this reminder, Hanani speaks the words in 2 Chronicles 16:9, telling him that God is looking to support those whose hearts are completely His. Hanani ended by saying King Asa acted foolishly and he would have many wars because of this. We experience all sorts of consequences for foolishly trusting in our own power and living with divided hearts. It may not be physical wars, but whatever consequences we face remind us of our failure to love God with wholehearted devotion. What happened to King Asa? As John warns us of the church in Ephesus, he lost his first love (Revelation 2:4-5). It was a slow erosion, one division at a time.

A Heart That's Completely His

> "I acknowledge my sin to you, and I did not cover my iniquity;
> I said, 'I will confess my transgressions to the LORD,' and you forgave the iniquity of my sin." Psalm 32:5

The heart that is God's completely is the only heart that can fear Him. It is an undivided heart with single devotion to God, entirely and continually surrendered to Him. No person in our flesh can have this heart. It is only possible through a relationship with Jesus Christ who gives "strong support" to us through the Holy Spirit. When we abide in Him, He keeps our hearts united in the fear of the LORD.

David was known as a man after God's own heart. Looking at his life in the pages of Scripture, we find his life was not the most righteous but rather full of sins and shortcomings. Some may look at the list of sins and think, "There's no way this guy's heart was completely the Lord's." For those who look strictly at the sins, yes, he failed many times over but his response to his sins set him apart as a man after God's own heart. He grieved over his sin because it dishonored the Lord. That grief led to repentance, a turning back of his heart from all the divided affections to that single, God-focused love and reverence.

We often share verses about confessing our sins when someone first understands the gospel and God's desire to be in a right relationship with us. Because God is holy and cannot commune with the unholy, we must be made righteous. When we confess our sins to Him, believing Jesus cleanses us and gives us His righteousness, we are saved. We must also remember that our confession of sin should be a continual act, not to be justified again because we have already been given eternal life, but so we continue to offer our bodies as living sacrifices, holy and pleasing to God because this is our spiritual act of worship (Romans 12:1). When confessing our sins, we turn our lives back over to God, and more specifically our hearts, back to God saying, "Take my heart. It is yours, not mine. I know that from my heart flows everything else and I want what flows from it to be pleasing to you." David's life was marked by continually returning his heart to God; this should not be the exception for a believer in Jesus Christ, but the norm.

If this is the norm for a follower of Jesus Christ, it should cause us fear and trembling as we look over our days and evaluate our lives. We should not justify our sins or ignore them, nor should they cripple us. Knowing God will draw near to us anytime we draw near to Him (James 4:8), that very kindness should lead us to repentance and a renewed dependence on His grace and mercy. By doing this, we acknowledge that in our own power, we could never have a heart that is completely His without His help. And all praise to Him as He gives us that help, freely and abundantly, if we simply ask Him.

A Heart of Flesh

> "And I will give you a new heart, and put a new spirit in you; I will remove from you your heart of stone and give you a heart of flesh." Ezekiel 36:26 (NIV)

As a young Christian, I was so confused by this verse because in the New Testament, "flesh" is negative, referring to our sinful nature. In Ezekiel 36, we see God removing a heart of stone and giving us a heart of flesh. It did not make sense. I have since learned more about this verse in the context of Scripture. The Bible often warns of hardened hearts. In Hebrews, the Preacher tells us not to be hardened by the deceitfulness of sin (Hebrews 3:13). The more comfortable we are with our sin, the more we are deceived by it, and the harder our hearts become. The reverse is also true: The more we grieve our sin, the more aware we are of how it impacts our relationship with God and others, and the softer and more sensitive our hearts become to sin. I believe this is what God means when He says He will give us a heart of flesh. It is a heart that is sensitive—sensitive to our sin, sensitive to the pain we face, sensitive to the pain others face, and sensitive to how our lives please God. "The closer we are to God, the more the slightest sin will cause us deep sorrow."[49] A heart that fears God is a sensitive and undivided heart that is interested in pleasing God as the Spirit leads. One of the most obvious and significant ways the Spirit works in our undivided hearts is to help us love Him and love others.

---

[49] Sproul, R. C. 2009. *Does Prayer Change Things?* Reformation Trust Publishing.

CHAPTER 20

The Greatest Commandment

"Jesus answered, 'The most important is, "Hear, O Israel: The Lord our God, the Lord is one. And you shall love the Lord your God with all your heart and with all your soul and with all your mind and with all your strength." The second is this: "You shall love your neighbor as yourself." There is no other commandment greater than these.'" Mark 12:29-31

"The first and great evidence of our walking by the Spirit or being filled with the Spirit is not some private mystical experience of our own, but our practical relationships of love with other people." John Stott[50]

The religious leaders had enough of Jesus; he destroyed their nice and neat religion with His words and deeds. Meanwhile, the people loved Him—not just any people, but sinners. The worst of the worst in the community drew near to Him. The shocking thing was that He would not shun them or condemn them. He would welcome and eat with them; this was not the way many of the religious leaders dealt with sinners. He was causing much unrest for them, and they needed to restrain Him so He wouldn't continue to gain popularity. They planned to trap Him with their questions about the Law confident He would say something heretical because they felt He was obviously living contrary to the Law by treating sinners as He did. "If He really loved God, He would not act that way. He would act like us," they likely mused. But every time they tried to trap Him, He would only confirm what they believed, expose their lack of understanding about the Law, or

---

[50] Stott, John R. W. 1984. *The Message of Galatians*. InterVarsity Press.

their failure to keep it. They hated Him for it and grew increasingly angry, resentful, and more determined to get rid of Him.

Days before Jesus's crucifixion, there was a final exchange between Him and a curious scribe. The scribe asked Jesus which commandment was the most important (Mark 12:28). Surely, this would be challenging. There were over 600 laws, and all of God's laws were important, or He would not have commanded them.

Love is the Right Answer

> "Hear, O Israel: The LORD our God, the LORD is one. You shall love the LORD your God with all your heart and with all your soul and with all your might. And these words that I command you today shall be on your heart." Deuteronomy 6:4-6

As He had done in the past, Jesus confirmed what they believed to be true. He quoted from the Torah (Deuteronomy and Leviticus, specifically). He recited what they recited three times a day, the Shema. The scribe affirmed Jesus's response with a tone of authority as if to say, "Good boy, Jesus, you are right to say there is no other God, so you cannot be whom you say you are." But Jesus responded with the authority the scribes and religious leaders thought belonged to them. Jesus clarified to the scribe, who was so confident in the law, that *he* was almost there in his understanding. Jesus was instructing him, not the other way around. "And when Jesus saw that he answered wisely, He said to him, 'You are not far from the kingdom of God'" (Mark 12:34). Jesus confirmed that the scribe's response was correct, but he was the one who needed to examine his heart and submit to the authority of God instead of his own. He was close to the kingdom of God but the chasm that separated him from it was love.

Love for the Right God

What can we learn from this exchange as we seek to love God as He commands? Jesus didn't begin His response with, "You shall love the Lord your God with all your heart and with all your soul and with all your mind and with all your strength…and you shall love your neighbor as yourself." He tracked back to the beginning of the Shema, acknowledging that "the LORD our God, the LORD is one." What makes this significant is that Jesus reminds the scribe what he needs to know first: To love the LORD your God with all your heart and with all your soul and with all your mind and with all your strength, you must first know God is One. This knowledge is the foundation upon which our love for Him is built. Jesus speaks of God as being first and above all earthly gods (idols). But it could also be that Jesus is speaking of the Trinity, declaring God is three in one: Father, Son, and Holy Spirit. To obey the greatest commandment, you must first love the One True God, believing He is not only God the Father but also God the Son and God the Holy Spirit. Believing in God without Jesus Christ or the Holy Spirit channels affection to an idol. Believing God is three in one is the first step in the right direction.

Believing the truth of the Trinity means we have the power to obey God through the Holy Spirit because of Jesus Christ. After His atoning death on the cross and His resurrection from the dead, He told His disciples He was leaving but sending a Helper (John 14:16). The Holy Spirit is our Helper, equipping us to obey the greatest commandment and guaranteeing our sanctification in this life as we do so. What does it look like for the Holy Spirit to help us love the LORD with all our heart, soul, mind, and strength? It looks like holiness, the life of Jesus. When we live as Jesus Christ lived, we are yielded to the Spirit as He displays the fruit of our love for God in every aspect of our lives (heart, soul, mind, strength). When we live contrary to how Christ lived, we live in disobedience to God and His commands.

All of our Everything

To expound in detail on what it looks like to love God with each part of our being would take much more than part of a single chapter. In a sense, that is what this book means to accomplish as we look at fearing God with our lives. While we can look at each aspect of the command in sections, we must acknowledge that they are not divisible. As the previous chapter explained, we are to love God with an undivided heart. But not just an undivided heart but an undivided soul, mind, and every bit of our energy and giftings. Our love for God must include all of our heart, all of our soul, all of our mind, and all of our strength. To lack one part would be failing to keep the greatest commandment. Yet again, we encounter an unattainable goal, at least in our own power. On our own, we make poor attempts to love God with our feeble hearts, fickle souls, flippant minds, and failing strength. We need God to accomplish in us what we cannot do ourselves.

Loving All of God

R. C. Sproul shared about a time one of his students entered his classroom with a beaming smile and a sparkle on her hand. A young man entered after her. Dr. Sproul asked if she had become engaged to this young man and she confirmed the good news. He began a brief question-and-answer session with the young woman in front of the class. He asked her why she loved John. She thought about it and gave the first response: "He is so smart." Dr. Sproul agreed with her statement but argued that another young man in the class had an even higher GPA. "There must be something in John that you love that's not in Bill. What is it?" he asked again. She replied a second time, "John is so athletic." Dr. Sproul agreed again listing the sports John played and his many accomplishments but commented that Bill was the high scorer and captain of the team. After being asked a third time, the young lady said her fiancé was so polite and courteous. Dr. Sproul jokingly turned to Bill and asked, "Did you hear that, Bill? Are you rude?" The young lady realized her response did not set her fiancé apart and made it seem like all other men, including Bill, qualified for her love. What was it that made her love John above all other men? After becoming increasingly nervous, she stuttered through her words, searching for why her love for John was unique and replied with frustration and conviction: "I love him because he is John!" "Yes," Dr. Sproul replied.

While John had many wonderful qualities, the best way she knew to sum up the essence of who he was, this one man she loved, was to say his name. In his name, she found his entire being and his total uniqueness. She could not separate his characteristics or abilities because they made up a unique and complex person she came to know and love—someone unlike any other.

We struggle to articulate our love for God. Sometimes we become confused and short-sighted when people ask why we love God. We begin naming His qualities, what He can do, or the blessings He gives us to explain why we love Him, but all of these fall short. They are incomplete responses to a profoundly deep question. Just as *we* are to love God in totality of heart, soul, mind, and strength, we are to love *God* in totality, without separating His being. Unless we can say we love God because he is God, He is worthy of our love and devotion, and we revere Him for all of who He is, not separating or omitting parts of His character, because in doing so He would cease to be God, then we don't love Him. We are to love God completely because He is completely God.

Why the Second Commandment?

Jesus curiously didn't name just one single command as the scribe requested. When He responded to the scribe, He included the second commandment. Why did Jesus take the time to include the second one? Jesus knew the necessary connection between the two. You cannot love God and hate your brother (1 John 4:20). The second command isn't an afterthought but a plumb line. By loving your neighbor, you prove your love for God. Our love for others is the manifestation of our love for God. He knew many scribes and Pharisees were too caught up in "loving" God to prove that love by loving their neighbor. They openly abhorred the disciples and others who followed Jesus, effectively nullifying their "love" for God.

A Weighty Call

Jesus is God. No one can fathom the majesty and transcendence of God and the weighty call to love Him, but Jesus can. When the scribe told Jesus he was right in stating that we are to love God with all our heart, soul, mind, and strength and love our neighbor as ourselves, Jesus was the only One who could actually do it. There stood the scribe, staring God right in the face and telling Him, as if he knew better, how to love.

Like the religious leaders, we try to love God and others according to His commands, but we fail. Every day, many times a day, if we're honest with ourselves, we need to confess our failed attempts to love God with our own efforts instead of His power or confess our outright disobedience and refusal to love Him because we want to remain in our sin for just a bit longer. Whatever the case, we fall short of this highest call to love God and others. The question is, how do we respond when we realize our failure to love God as called? Do we walk away from God and not ask any more questions, or do we turn back to Him and draw near to Him? God is gracious to us when we turn back to Him, no matter how many times we fail. It's not the number of times we turn back to Him that matters; it's the fact that we do.

CHAPTER 21

Second Chances

"Blessed be the God and Father of our Lord Jesus Christ! According to his great mercy, he has caused us to be born again to a living hope through the resurrection of Jesus Christ from the dead, to an inheritance that is imperishable, undefiled, and unfading..." 1 Peter 1:3-4

"They who truly come to God for mercy, come as beggars, and not as creditors: they come for mere mercy, for sovereign grace, and not for anything that is due." Jonathan Edwards[51]

I hated to read, a fact that didn't change until college. Book reports were possibly the worst assignments given in my educational career. My fourth-grade teacher was one of my favorite teachers but her greatest flaw was that she assigned book reports. Toward the end of the year, she assigned yet another book report. I was not interested in putting the work in for this one. Instead of reading the book *Little House on the Prairie*, I felt confident I could flip through the pages, look at the cover art and get a general idea. As I wrote the report, adding parts of sentences from the book, and naming characters mentioned in the story, I had this growing confidence that I would get by with this approach. I would fool her. Though she gave specific instructions at the beginning of the year on how to complete a book report, with step one being to read the book, I thought my way would work just as well. Her rules didn't matter as long as I had a "report" to show for it.

I turned in the book report. One afternoon later in the week, my mom said my teacher was coming over. She needed to talk to me about something.

---

[51] Edwards, Jonathan. 1974. *The Works of Jonathan Edwards*. Banner of Truth.

At that moment, I knew she knew. She was coming to my house to scold me for my failed attempt at tricking her. The minutes seemed like hours. Even the Lego house I was working on couldn't get my mind off the inevitable conversation. Then the waiting was over. Somehow, she ended up in my room. What I dreaded was true. She knew I had not read the book and she was disappointed. I was devastated. My sweet and funny teacher was serious in her tone. She gave me an assignment I failed to do according to her instructions, so I would receive a zero. If I wanted another chance, I could read the book and do the report again, the right way this time. I loved my teacher. I hated to disappoint her, and I was so grateful to have a second chance to do it right.

Did she lose "favorite teacher" status when she confronted me about my wrongdoing? No. In fact, that moment kept her in the running among the best. She didn't give me what I deserved the day she came to my house, and that event marked our relationship in a special way. For the rest of the year, I made every effort to please her, not because I was afraid of punishment, but because I was so grateful for her kindness. Because she loved me in my failure, I wanted to please her, to show my love for her in return. I knew I didn't deserve the second chance but receiving it changed everything that year.

A Son's Second Chance

> "Who is a God like you, pardoning iniquity and passing over transgression for the remnant of his inheritance? He does not retain his anger forever, because he delights in steadfast love."
> Micah 7:18

The parable of the prodigal son in Luke 15 is a story of love seen in second chances. Jesus tells the story while tax collectors and sinners draw near to hear, and the Pharisees and scribes grumble that He "receives sinners and eats with them" (Luke 15:1). He tells how the younger son selfishly asked for his inheritance before his father's death, taking it and squandering it all in a foreign land. He told them how the younger son ultimately found himself in a miserable state, longing to eat what pigs eat. The son realized the ridiculousness of his behavior as he remembered that even the servants of his father's house were well taken care of and never went hungry. When he faced the truth of his actions, which brought him to this sad and depressing place, and the truth of his father's great love for him, he was broken over what he had done. He repented and returned to his father. The father saw him far off, "ran and embraced him, and kissed him." The father told his servants to put the best robe on his son, put a ring on his hand, and kill the fattened calf so they could eat and celebrate.

Recalling the distinctions among forgiveness, repentance, and reconciliation, we notice each element in this parable. The son came to a place of brokenness and repentance over his sin. He committed in his heart to go to his father, saying, "I have sinned against heaven and before you." Before the son could apologize and humble himself, the father demonstrated his forgiveness from a distance, feeling compassion for him and running to him in love. The father's heart was full of forgiveness before he heard a word from his son's mouth. When repentance and forgiveness met, the result was reconciliation and restoration. The father and son celebrated his return!

Jesus spent significant time on the older brother's response to this second chance. Luke 15:28 says, "he was angry and refused to go in" to celebrate, so his father came out to him, calling on him to join them. The older son spoke disrespectfully to his father, certain he was making the wrong decision by taking the younger son back. He hated that his brother was getting a second chance. In his pride, the older brother felt entitled to the celebration his younger, undeserving brother received. He thought he earned it because he was a good son. He was so full of anger, pride, and jealousy, he had no room for gratitude and thankfulness to his father who said, "all that is mine is yours." The father gives his older son a final response. Not one of condemnation, but one of patient love as he told his indignant son one last time that it was fitting to celebrate and be glad that his lost brother returned.

The father was ready to welcome both sons into his home though both acted wrongly: the younger son's publicly shameful acts and the older son's private unforgiveness and pride. The younger son entered with his father, but the older son resisted going in to celebrate his brother's return. We are left to ask two questions: 1. What did the older brother do in the end? 2. Which brother am I? Am I the younger sinful brother who doesn't deserve a second chance, broken over my sin, and grieved that I disappointed my father? Or am I the older sinful brother who doesn't recognize my own need for a second chance?

Resenting Mercy and Grace

There is nothing new under the sun. Even today, we see a replication of the times of Jesus's public ministry and the establishment of the early church.

We have religious leaders in mind and heart, not necessarily in vocation, who would rather grumble about others' heinous offenses against God while boasting about their (self) righteousness than come meekly to the throne of grace to receive help in time of need. We can so easily think this way when we seemingly walk on the right path. We begin acting as though we don't need grace. It's all the other sinners who need it. We may look on skeptically when "major sinners" say they have turned to Christ. Our shock and skepticism really communicate, "My God is gracious, just not *that* gracious," which is the same attitude of the Pharisees, scribes, and older brother in the parable. The Pharisees felt they deserved God's goodness and favor because they were "good" sons who always stayed close to God and faithfully did what He wanted them to do. But even they failed to see that they, too, were undeserving. By not loving their neighbors, they failed to love God.

Jonah, a prophet of God, acted as the older brother when he refused to be used by God to bring the message of salvation to the Ninevites. God sovereignly overruled Jonah's desires and accomplished His good purposes anyway but Jonah was bitter and angry that God would give such an undeserving people such an undeserving gift (Jonah 4:1-2). But if we believe the gospel, we understand that we are the undeserving people receiving the undeserved gift. Paul came to realize this fact. He was one of the most qualified Jews who hated the "younger brothers" receiving grace while he worked a lifetime to earn God's favor, a futile endeavor. But God opened his eyes to see and know the truth of the gospel—none of us can attain a right standing with God apart from a relationship with Jesus Christ. And only when we come to God knowing and believing that truth will we receive that unmerited favor, that grace, that second chance (Ephesians 1:11-14).

Misunderstanding Mercy and Grace

> "Men will never worship God with a sincere heart, or be roused to fear and obey Him with sufficient zeal, until they properly understand how much they are indebted to His mercy." John Calvin[52]

We were driving home from church one afternoon when our daughter

---

[52] Calvin, John. 1995. *Calvin's New Testament Commentaries, Volume 8: Romans and Thessalonians.* Wm. B. Eerdmans-Lightning Source.

was asking if she could have a privilege that was recently taken away as a consequence. She asked, "Can't you just show me grace?" The previous month or so, we had been talking about grace. We explained it in various situations, including when we gave her a special privilege she did not deserve. Her question proved that she understood grace was undeserving but in asking for it, she showed us she was beginning to expect it. Her logic was that if she acted contrary to the way we wanted, she would receive a consequence, but then she could ask for grace every time.

I wonder if this is the state where modern Christianity finds itself today. Many have grown accustomed to hearing of God's grace, that He loves "unconditionally," so we feel we deserve it. But expecting grace regardless of godly sorrow over our sin is not biblical. God opposes the proud but gives grace to the humble (James 4:6). We cannot be proud and expect grace from God.

In the parable of the prodigal son, the father shows grace to the repentant younger brother who was willing to work as his servant, knowing he didn't deserve full restoration. The older brother wondered why he wasn't given a party and treated as wonderfully as the younger son, who acted so horribly. Unlike the younger brother, he thought he deserved that kind of treatment. But the older brother had it wrong. The older brother wasn't looking for grace; he was expecting what he thought he deserved for his work as an "obedient and faithful" son. Grace would have been disgusting to him. It would have implied that he failed. In our pride, that would make sense. In our flesh, we want the party, the robe, the ring, the feast, and the inheritance because we think we deserve it.

That day we had a good talk with our daughter about the unmerited favor that is grace. It comes to the humble and broken who know they don't deserve it, not to the proud who insist on it because they think they do (James 4:6). Neither son deserved an inheritance from their father. One cannot earn an inheritance; it is a gift based on a relationship. In the same way, none of us deserve the inheritance God gives His children. It is a gracious gift we receive by faith in Christ, without merit of our own; this is what makes it so shocking and why the proud are indignant about it. Grace restores what would otherwise be broken forever; unless it is broken, there is nothing for grace to restore.

Restoration Through Second Chances

> "God uses broken things. It takes broken soil to produce a crop, broken clouds to give rain, broken grain to give bread, broken bread to give strength. It is the broken alabaster box that gives forth perfume... it is Peter, weeping bitterly, who returns to greater power than ever." Vance Havner[53]

Jesus delights in restoring broken things. We see this throughout the gospels. We, too, should delight in God's power and grace to restore broken things: broken people, relationships, and cultures. And what a privilege it is that we can be agents of that restoration as we extend mercy and grace to those around us. The picture of the father and younger son celebrating his return is a beautiful picture of restoration that we can experience through Jesus Christ when we come to Him in our brokenness. In contrast, the image of the father beckoning to his indignant older son demonstrates how pride can destroy relationships, most significantly a relationship with a loving Father who desires to show us all His mercy and grace if we humble ourselves before Him.

Our world today is sick and sad. We all need the love of God, and He means for us to manifest His love through mercy and grace toward one another. When we live in love, then all men will know we are disciples of Jesus Christ. Love proves our right and holy fear of the One True God, and He works in mighty ways through His love.

---

[53] Havner, Vance. 1934. *The Still Water.* Fleming H. Revell.

PART V

Obedience and the Fear of God

CHAPTER 22

The Whole Duty of Man

"The end of the matter: all has been heard. Fear God and keep his commandments, for this is the whole duty of man." Ecclesiastes 12:13

"On the day of Judgment, it will be demanded of us not what we have read, but what we have done." Thomas à Kempis[54]

"I did it, mama!" My preschool-age son was learning how to do chores. We started with setting the table, a job his older sister was thrilled to pass down. He had just finished putting the silverware on top of the placemats. I could tell by his smile and the sparkle in his eye that he was so pleased. It wasn't just the completed task that he was proud of but the fact that he knew how pleased we would be with his efforts.

We had seen this reaction a few times in the recent past: when he picked up his toys as we asked him to do, when he did his best coloring, or when he shared a toy he wanted to keep for himself. We would celebrate his obedience, and our pleasure would increase his joy. And although it wasn't a conscious recognition on his part, we could see that gleam in his eyes when he knew he was doing the exact thing we wanted him to do. It delighted him that he delighted us.

We teach our children what to do because we love them and know what is best for them. Our motive is not to ruin their lives; it is quite the opposite. We want them to thrive within the boundaries we have established in our home. When they submit to our rules and boundaries and fulfill their responsibilities, it makes for a happy home; the kids are happy, and the parents are happy. In the same way, God has given us His good will for our lives. We

---

[54] À Kempis, Thomas. 2003. *The Imitation of Christ.* Dover Publications.

can live according to that guidance given in His Word and written on our hearts, or we can live contrary to it. When we submit joyfully to His moral will (obedience), we experience His goodness and grace as it abounds in our lives. My son experienced that joy by fulfilling the work we had for him to do. Setting the table was his duty, and he was pleased to please us by doing it.

Our Duty in Life

Duty has been conspicuously absent from American vocabulary. Dictionaries add and omit words every year based on increased or decreased usage. Still, even without the formal removal of words, we can see what is valuable to a culture and what is repugnant to it based on word trends. It's not surprising, then, that duty, defined as "a moral or legal obligation; a responsibility," is not referenced much in our culture today. It is not valuable to the world. In fact, it is a concept more and more people are rejecting. Everything about duty seems to go against our self-focused culture. Every word in its definition is looked down on or considered irrelevant: moral, legal, obligation, responsibility. Today's culture has moved so far from values to do with morals, law, commitment, and responsibility that it's no wonder duty is nearly non-existent in both word and practice.

While the world tries to deny or downplay the significance of duty, Scripture tells us many times over of its importance. God's Word even tells us that humanity was created to fulfill a specific duty. So, not only is duty a necessary part of our lives, but our response to this specific duty is also the single greatest factor that shapes our eternal lives. We either accept the duty for which we were made or reject it. Solomon closes the book of Ecclesiastes with a summation of his many words, warnings, and instructions. If you read no other part of Ecclesiastes, he tells us this is the most important takeaway: "The end of the matter; all has been heard. Fear God and keep his commandments, for this is the whole duty of man" (Ecclesiastes 12:13).

Fearing God is our duty. We were made to fear God and obey Him, this is our singular purpose. They are named separately, but they are inseparable. You cannot fear God if you don't obey Him, and you cannot obey God if you don't fear Him. Obedience to God is synonymous with fearing Him in the same way that loving God is synonymous with fearing Him. Love, obedience, and fear overlap in so many ways that it's unreasonable to describe a Christian using one of the words absent from the others. According to His Word, our love and obedience manifest our fear, honor, and reverence. We see over and over in Scripture statements that tie together love, obedience, and fear (Deuteronomy 5:29, Deuteronomy 6:24, Psalm 112:1, Matthew 7:24, John 14:15, John 14:23). Obedience is the evidence of our love and fear of God and proof that we belong to Him.

Blessing for Fear

> "The LORD has remembered us; he will bless us; he will bless the house of Israel; he will bless the house of Aaron; he will bless those who fear the LORD, both the small and the great." Psalm 115:12-13

Scripture connects love, obedience, and fear with one other concept: Blessing. God promises great joy and blessing to those who fear and obey Him. Do not understand this blessing as ease in life, fame, wealth, or popularity. Blessing from God is always according to His riches in Christ Jesus. He blesses us with every spiritual blessing (Ephesians 1:3), with eternal life through our obedience to God and fearing Him (Proverbs 10:27; 19:23, Proverbs 22:4), and for our good always (Deuteronomy 6:24). Those who obey Him are His prized possession (Deuteronomy 12:28); they are blessed (Psalm 112:1, Psalm 115:13, Psalm 128:2-4, Proverbs 28:14) because He saves them (Psalm 34:7, Psalm 85:9, Psalm 145:19). As we fulfill our purpose, our lives will reflect the blessing that comes from our submission to God.

In contrast, should we reject our duty to fear God and keep His commands we will receive the just consequences for our defiance of Him (Deuteronomy 8:20). Our response to this solemn duty to fear God touches everything in our lives.

When we fear God and obey His commandments, we acknowledge He is our authority. We submit to Him and respect His rule and reign in our lives. The world and our flesh despise these three components, authority, submission, and respect, that are necessary for obedience.

Authority, Submission, and Respect

> "'O LORD, God of our fathers, are you not God in heaven? You rule over all the kingdoms of the nations. In your hand are power and might, so that none is able to withstand you.'" 2 Chronicles 20:6

According to Oxford Languages, authority means "the power or right to give orders, make decisions, and enforce obedience." The problem with authority is that it implies submission. By acknowledging someone has authority over us, we admit our lowly position under them, contrary to our natural desire to rule. The world hates authority unless they are their own authority. They want to be in charge. They want power to rule over themselves, so they refuse to submit to the orders of others. This power struggle is the default setting of every human being. Our sinful nature, our flesh, wants to live in self-focused fear with reverence and authority reserved for ourselves, not others, and certainly not God. In our flesh, we feel threatened by authority because if we submit to it, we relinquish our control and power to that authority. But we fail to realize we never had control. That always has, and always will, belong to God alone.

God is the ruler of all things and acts according to His will (Psalm 115:3, Job 23:13, Job 42:2, Psalm 135:6, Isaiah 46:10, Ephesians 1:11). He alone is in charge, so our duty is to fear and obey Him. He has ultimate authority, and He is worthy of our submission. We submit to His commands and plans for our lives because we love Him, and He is good. Even if we refuse to submit, He still has authority over our lives and will judge us according to our submission or defiance to Him as King of kings and Lord of lords. Consider the very last verse of Ecclesiastes: "For God will bring every deed into judgment, with every secret thing, whether good or evil." Whether we submit to His rightful authority or not, God has not ceased to be God because we have rejected His commands and the duty He has given us. He knows whether we have obeyed Him with a heart of reverent respect, with the honor due His name, or if we have acted for our own benefit and glory apart from Him.

Our Duty and the Greatest Commandment

> "Owe no one anything, except to love each other, for the one who loves another has fulfilled the law." Romans 13:8

Sometimes Christians can focus on an abstract idea of fearing God as if it is only a private internal work between God and us. While it is an internal work, it's worth emphasizing that Jesus connected "love your neighbor as yourself" with "love the LORD your God with all your heart and with all your soul and with all your mind and with all your strength." "There is no commandment [singular] greater than these" (Mark 12:30-31). Jesus tells us that our love for Him and one another are intricately connected. In fact, our love for one another proves our love for Him (John 13:35). How does this relate to our duty? Loving God and one another *is* our duty. We show that we fear God by obeying His commands, and His greatest commandment is to love Him completely and love one another. Our reverent and respectful submission to His authority is not strictly relegated to our relationship with Him but it is evidenced in our relationships with one another. We are to serve one another as we serve Him.

Consider this point related to submission: We do not submit to God in some abstract way. We submit to Him very practically as we obey His Word which includes commands to submit to governing authorities (Titus 3:1), submit to leaders in the church (Hebrews 13:17), wives submit to husbands (Ephesians 5:22,24), submit to one another (Ephesians 5:21), submit to every human authority (1 Peter 2:13-14). These commands don't contradict God's command to submit to Him; they are some practical ways we do submit to Him. When we submit to human authority for the Lord's sake (1 Peter 2:13), we honor and fear Him. We love Him and each other.

Joyfully Accepting Our Duty

> "True Christians consider themselves not as satisfying some rigorous Creator, but as discharging a debt of gratitude."
> William Wilberforce[55]

Although duty brings with it obligation, a Christian's duty is not slavish as we tend to think of it. It is a reverent duty. We fear and obey God out of love and reverence for Him, not as robots or slaves afraid of what might happen if we disobey the dictator. Instead, we accept this duty as children honoring our Father, who has proven His love for us. We accept this duty because we trust He is good and loving. What God commands us to do is not at our expense and His pleasure but for our good and His glory. With that child-like faith, we joyfully accept our duty to fear Him and keep His commandments. Just as my precious son found joy in his good work because it delighted us, we too find joy in doing all God commands us to do because it pleases Him.

---

[55] Wilberforce, William. 2005. *Real Christianity: Discerning True Faith from False Beliefs*. COOK, David C.

CHAPTER 23

The Significance of the Law

"For God has done what the law, weakened by the flesh, could not do. By sending his own Son in the likeness of sinful flesh and for sin, he condemned sin in the flesh, in order that the righteous requirement of the law might be fulfilled in us, who walk not according to the flesh but according to the Spirit." Romans 8:3-4

"There is no fulfillment of the law apart from communion with God, and no communion with God apart from fulfillment of the law… Only the doer of the law can remain in communion with Jesus." Dietrich Bonhoeffer[56]

Obedience to God's commandments, or His law, marks those who fear Him. The law is not an irrelevant topic as many, even in churches, claim. It's not hard to find people brushing off God's commands with an argument that grace supersedes all. Understanding the law and its importance is part of understanding grace and our new lives in Christ. How can we understand obedience to God, the whole duty of man, apart from His law? Is His law not what He commands us to obey? Still, many push it aside for various reasons: it's boring, irrelevant, or harsh. The list goes on.

God's law can only be boring, irrelevant, and harsh to the one who doesn't know it. The one who knows it longs to understand it better, to obey it more completely, and delight in it more faithfully (Psalm 1:2). David declared, "I delight to do Your will, O my God; Your law is within my heart" (Psalm 40:8). He also said, "I shall delight in Your statutes; I shall not forget Your Word" (Psalm 119:16). Paul agreed with David when He said, "I delight in the law

---

[56] Bonhoeffer, Dietrich. 1995. *The Cost of Discipleship*. Simon and Schuster New York.

of God according to the inward man (Romans 7:22). If we aren't delighting in it, maybe we don't really understand it.

Understanding the Law

> "The man who does not know the nature of the Law, cannot know the nature of sin." John Bunyan[57]

Depending on the context, "the Law" can refer to the Ten Commandments, the first five books of the Bible (the Torah), or Old Testament Scriptures in general. Whether referenced in the Old or New Testament, the law typically speaks of God's commands—what He requires His people to do.

The commandments given by God in His Word are not suggestions but requirements. We read many times over about "keeping" the law or "doing" what it says (Leviticus 18:5, Deuteronomy 4:1, Deuteronomy 8:1, Psalm 119:17, Proverbs 4:4, Proverbs 7:2, Matthew 19:17, Romans 10:5, Galatians 3:12, James 1:22). It's not an occasional recommendation but a frequently stated expectation. With this constant emphasis on obeying God's law, why would the Christian love it? Why would it not be something we look on with disdain and irritation as a burden instead of a delight?

Why the Law?

> "What then shall we say? That the law is sin? By no means! Yet if it had not been for the law, I would not have known sin. For I would not have known what it is to covet if the law had not said, 'You shall not covet.'" Romans 7:7

Before meeting my husband, I had no interaction with choirs and conductors. Naturally, with no choral experience, I joined the choir a few months after we met. As an inexperienced chorister, who also happens to be married to the conductor, I have learned many things about conductors over the years. I have learned that, while not true of all conductors, the best conductors aim for perfection. I may be biased but I think he is one of the best. My husband's role as the conductor includes introducing the choir and orchestra to new music, teaching them the music, correcting them, and helping them make the intended

---

[57] Reisinger, Ernie. 2021. *The Law and the Gospel*. Founders Press.

sounds the composer had in mind. He aims to prepare them well, so they sing or play their part perfectly.

There are many errors during the choir's first introduction to the music. If we do not recognize the errors ourselves and correct them, the conductor points them out. Once we know what we are doing wrong, he expects us to correct those errors. The purpose of calling the errors out is not to shame us or personally attack us, nor is it meant to tear us down. The purpose of pointing out our errors is to make the errors known so we can make the wrong right as we work toward the goal of singing the song perfectly.

Just as the music instructs us on what to sing, the law instructs us on how to please God. Both our music and God's law instruct us, but they also show us when we miss the mark. Without the music, we wouldn't know what to sing and we wouldn't know when we were wrong. Without the law, we wouldn't know God's expectations and we wouldn't know when we were in sin. The music reveals to us the composer's expectations and the law reveals God's expectation—perfect obedience. It is an impossible standard.

The Challenge for the Jewish Leaders

> "For whoever keeps the whole law but fails in one point has become guilty of all of it." James 2:10

No one could keep the law perfectly, but the law was for God's people to obey. Many Jewish leaders perceived this perfect obedience to the law as a challenge instead of an impossibility. Having wrestled with the same struggle before God saved him, Paul could reason with these Jewish leaders better than anyone. He knew the demands of their traditions. He understood their enslavement to the law. As long as they viewed the law as a challenge to be accepted—a "to-do" list to accomplish—they condemned themselves because it was an impossible feat. Even if they only failed to keep one law, that would be enough to condemn them (James 2:10).

During the establishment of the early church, the disciples and apostles proclaimed the gospel of Jesus Christ to the Jews as the only hope for salvation. Many received the truth, but those who rejected it did so because Jesus was a stumbling block for them; this was especially the case for many Jewish leaders. They could not figure how a relationship with God wasn't because of works of the flesh but through faith in Jesus Christ whose Spirit works through those who believe. These leaders grew up with their religion. It was their identity. They heard the stories and memorized much of the law. They were bound to the traditions of the law and confident in their longstanding "good work" that earned them positions of high stature. They couldn't understand how none of that could save them.

Today we are dealing with the same struggles in our own churches. The tradition of religion has become an identity to many. Church is something they do instead of who they are as the Bride of Christ. The blessings that come with growing up in church are abundant, and hearing the truth from a young age can set us on the right track for the rest of our lives. Still, we must be careful not to elevate our traditions, positions, and reputations above our relationship with Jesus Christ. For many people today, their definition of salvation is precisely what many Jewish leaders said defined their relationship with God—their hard work (keeping the law according to their standards). As Paul pleaded with them to give up their works of the flesh and turn to Christ, the Spirit pleads with us to renounce all ties to anything but Jesus, who alone made the impossible possible.

The Gift of the Law

> "You search the Scriptures because you think that in them you have eternal life; and it is they that bear witness about me," John 5:39

To many people, the Bible is a book full of rules they must obey. While this is not necessarily incorrect, it is incomplete. God commands us to keep His law, but when we look at the law rightly, realizing the impossibility of keeping it, we must look beyond ourselves. We cannot please God by our own means. We need help. The Bible tells us over and over how we fall short of God's expectation, but it also tells us over and over of the One who made the impossible possible—the One who did what none of us could do, the One who kept God's law perfectly and made a way for His people to stand justified before God.

When Jesus came, He didn't change or reject God's law as if all the commandments from the Old Testament were irrelevant once He showed up. Jesus tells us He came to fulfill the law (Matthew 5:17). He obeyed every word of God's commands and demonstrated that perfect obedience in our stead. He lived the perfect life that pleased God by keeping the whole law, and showed us God's expectation for His people. Jesus is the manifestation of the law for us. He is the image of the invisible God (Colossians 1:15).

He wasn't only perfectly obedient in everyday life, but he was perfectly obedient even to the point of death on a cross (Philippians 2:8). His death and resurrection were why He didn't come into the world to condemn it but to save it (John 3:16-17). If He had lived perfectly to show us how we are supposed to live but never died, He would have only been a perfect example who left us hopelessness because of our sins. He would have only shown us how we miss the mark of perfect obedience. But God loved us. He didn't stop there. He graciously gave up His own Son for us all (Romans 8:32). "God demonstrated His love for us in that while we were still sinners Christ died for us" (Romans 5:8). He sent Jesus to keep the law, glorifying God, but He also sent Him to die to pay the punishment for all our sins. This payment was necessary for us to have a right relationship with God, since only those who keep God's law perfectly can be in His holy presence. Jesus took our sins on Him in His death so that those who believe in His death and resurrection could have His righteousness (2 Corinthians 5:21). His perfect obedience becomes ours; His holy life is lived out in those who believe and abide in Him today.

The Purpose of the Law

> "...the commandments are not given inappropriately or pointlessly; but in order that through them the proud, blind man may learn the plague of his impotence, should he try to do as he is commanded." Martin Luther[58]

It was right after God delivered the Ten Commandments that Moses said to the Israelites, "Do not fear, for God has come to test you, that the fear of Him may be before you, that you may not sin" (Exodus 20:20). God gave us the law, not so that we would try to keep it ourselves nor to be terrified of His just consequences, but to see our failure to pass the test of perfect obedience and turn to Him. When we look into the law and see our failure to pass the test, our only hope is to look to the only One who accomplished what the law required and ask Him for help. Jesus gives us this help in the Person of the Holy Spirit who fills us with the fear of the Lord, a joyful reverence in our

---

[58] Luther, Martin. 2012. *The Bondage of the Will.* Translated by J. I. Packer, and O. R. Johnston. Baker Academic.

submission to our loving God. This fear of the Lord keeps us from sin as we keep the law in His power and for His glory.

Your Law Within My Heart

> "For this is the covenant that I will make with the house of Israel after those days, declares the LORD: I will put my law within them, and I will write it on their hearts. And I will be their God, and they shall be my people." Jeremiah 31:33

Both David and Paul acknowledged that the law was in their hearts. How can external laws God commands like "do not murder" or "have no idols," be in our hearts? The Bible talks about the works of the law being written on every heart, even on the hearts of those who don't love God (Romans 2:14-15), but this law in the heart of those who delight in God is only within the hearts of God's people. It is Christ, the fulfillment of the law, in us (Colossians 1:27). When we trust Christ took our sin and believe that we must rest in His righteousness alone for salvation, His Spirit empowers us to do what God commands. When we fail to yield to the Spirit in obedience to God's law, He pricks our hearts. He tells us we are guilty when we gossip, steal, lust, and murder. He does this for the same purpose as the external law: to turn us back to Christ.

In our pride, it can be easy to push aside the Spirit's pricking, or conviction, by thinking, "Well, I didn't mean to do that" or "It's not that big a deal." These thoughts in our flesh lead us away from God. They make light of the weight of our sins. The Spirit convicts us for our good. He points out our failure to keep God's law in the flesh, so we will return to Jesus and say, "I'm sorry. I need help. I can't please you by keeping the law without you." God never turns us away when we do this. He receives us every time. With Christ commanding our hearts, we turn away from our sins with His power to obey all He commands.

CHAPTER 24

Confronting Our Disobedience

"[God] disciplines us for our good, that we may share in his holiness. For the moment all discipline seems painful rather than pleasant, but later it yields the peaceful fruit of righteousness to those who have been trained by it." Hebrews 12:10-11

"If my ruling disposition is self-interest, I perceive that everything that happens to me is always for or against my self-interest; if, on the other hand, my ruling disposition is obedience to God, I perceive Him to be working for my perfecting in everything that happens to me." Oswald Chambers[59]

What happens when we disobey God's commands? Because we are sinners, this is not a hypothetical question but an inevitable reality. It is something we don't often think about. We might think about it with a lopsided view of God, leaning heavily on His love and mercy but forsaking His justice and holiness. If we're honest with ourselves, we know we fail to meet God's standard of perfect obedience. When we sin, we cannot "unsin." We are quick to assert God's forgiveness, but we neglect another weighty aspect of our disobedience—the consequences of our sin and God's discipline.

The issue for Christians has never been who obeys the most perfectly. Jesus Christ is the One who accomplished perfect obedience in all God's children. Instead, the issue is how we respond when confronted with our disobedience. While obedience to God's law marks those who fear Him, how we respond when we fail to obey also distinguishes between those who fear

---

[59] Chambers, Oswald. 1998. *Biblical Ethics / The Moral Foundations of Life / The Philosophy of Sin: Ethical Principles of the Christian Life.* Discovery House.

God and those who don't. What do we do when we face our sin and experience the consequences for our sin and God's discipline?

The Right Response

> "Have mercy on me, O God, according to your steadfast love; according to your abundant mercy blot out my transgressions… Create in me a clean heart, O God, and renew a right spirit within me." Psalm 51:1, 10

Scripture repeatedly confirms that no one is without sin. We can look at Christ's genealogy alone and be shocked by two things: the magnitude of their sins and the magnitude of God's grace. The point cannot be emphasized enough—it is not that God's chosen people never sin (Paul said himself he was the worst of sinners). The point is that they are marked by how they respond to their sin. The Bible includes numerous true stories of people responding rightly or wrongly to their sin and their disobedience of God's law.

After King David committed adultery and murdered to cover it up, the LORD sent Nathan, the prophet, to confront him (2 Samuel 12). Nathan told him how he broke God's laws (2 Samuel 12:9) and explained the consequences for his sin (2 Samuel 12:10). David grieved over his sin, confessing it was against God alone whom he sinned (Psalm 51:2). He was broken over his sin not because he was caught but because he recognized what he had done—he sinned against God Almighty, the Holy One. He didn't deny the temporal consequences but received them as good discipline from the LORD, knowing He disciplines His children for their good—their holiness (Hebrews 12:10-11).

Right and Wrong Sacrifices

> "Those whom I love, I reprove and discipline, so be zealous and repent." Revelation 3:19

Near the end of David's psalm of lament, he acknowledged that "the sacrifices of God are a broken spirit; a broken and contrite heart, O God, you will not despise" (Psalm 51:17). Our sinful nature can't understand how that can be enough. We attempt to make up for our sins by doing something good, as if we will cancel the negative with a positive. When we hurt a friend and know we were wrong, we might try to make it up to them instead of apologizing. Doing good, as God declares it, is not bad, but if our purpose for "doing good" is to negate the sin we committed, or make us feel better, it doesn't do what we ultimately want it to do which is to remove our guilt. David knew he couldn't make up for his sin by offering a sacrifice as a token apology. It came down to the state of his heart, something he could not change unless God interceded. External works alone, like sacrifices or burnt offerings, or for us today, "nice deeds" to negate the bad, do not please God (Psalm 51:16) because they do not fix the problem in the heart. David understood this and demonstrated a right response to his sin: confession, repentance, and giving over his broken heart to God, who could renew it. David's right response is what God wants from us and what He wants to do in us. He delights in redeeming us and transforming us, but we must give the right sacrifice to him—a broken and contrite heart. No matter how many times we go through this process, or even if we go through it only once as our last dying breath, as the thief on the cross did (Luke 23:40-43), this response marks God's people who fear Him.

We do not always respond like this, and many never do. Our pride often keeps us from responding this way. Scripture shows us many examples of those who failed to respond rightly in their exposed disobedience. These stories can serve as warnings to us. We can confess our sins and receive God's discipline and temporal consequences, knowing they are for our good. Alternatively, we can reject His discipline and hate the temporal consequences knowing we will face eternal judgment for our sins.

The Wrong Response

> "And when they were in the field, Cain rose up against his brother Abel and killed him. Then the LORD said to Cain, 'Where is Abel your brother?' He said, 'I do not know; am I my brother's keeper?' And the LORD said, 'What have you done?'" Genesis 4:8-10

As individuals living in the world today, we don't want to take ownership and responsibility for anything, especially our sins. We get angry when people confront us; we want to blame our sins on others and try to find ways to avoid consequences at all costs. Both Cain and Abel offered sacrifices to God. One did so obediently, and one did so disobediently. When God confronted Cain with his disobedience, he got angry (Genesis 4:5). He wanted to obey God on his own terms and hated God for rejecting what he thought was a good sacrifice. God's reason for confronting Cain was not hate but love. God told him how he could be accepted (Genesis 4:7), giving Cain a second chance, but Cain refused again to do what God commanded. His anger festered. It grew into hatred and jealousy toward his brother, whom God accepted. Instead of ruling over his sin, sin ruled over him, and he murdered Abel.

Again, God was patient with Cain and didn't cast him out immediately for his disobedience, though He could have. He approached him as He approached Adam and Eve when they sinned, giving Cain the opportunity to expose and confess his sin. God still loved Cain, even knowing his sin. He wanted to be in a right relationship with Cain, but that meant Cain had to confess and turn from his sin. Cain foolishly lied to God and denied his sin. He demonstrated the many wrong ways we respond to our disobedience: anger, rejection of God's correction and instruction, lack of repentance, lying, justifying, blaming, and denying sin. Cain did not see God's confrontation as a gracious thing, a second chance, an opportunity to start fresh as David did. God confronts us when we sin to turn our hearts from disobedience to obedience so that we can be in a right relationship with Him and His people. How we respond makes all the difference.

Receiving vs. Rejecting Consequences

> "Real repentance means coming not only to be sorry for the consequences of sin but to hate sin itself." William Barclay[60]

David trusted God's goodness in His discipline and received His temporal consequences while Cain tried to escape the consequences of his disobedience. We have the choice to respond either way, as well. We can confess our sins and turn from them as David did, or we can respond like Cain with anger and denial. We think by denying our sin we avoid the consequences, but if we continue to do that, we are only delaying the consequences. Running from our sin, hiding it, or destroying the evidence of our sin may fool men but it

---

[60] Barclay, William. 2014. *Barclay on the Lectionary: Mark, Year B*. Hymns Ancient & Modern Ltd.

will not fool God. The verse following Solomon's summary statement on the whole duty of man warns of this truth: "For God will bring every deed into judgment, with every secret sin, whether good or evil" (Ecclesiastes 12:14). Whatever sins we try to hide, God sees. If we never confess our sins, they still belong to us and we will pay those wages. If we do not submit to Christ as Lord and confess our sins to Him, we will face His judgment. But that is not the only option, nor is it what God desires (2 Peter 3:9). Our only hope is payment for our sins and supernatural surgery that inserts righteousness where before there was sin upon sin upon sin. When we give our sin to God by confession and repentance, believing the wages of those sins were paid by the death of Jesus Christ, the result is that supernatural surgery.

God wants to save us. He is patient with us, delaying judgment so that we might repent. When we confess and repent, that sin is no longer ours. We have turned it over to God, who nailed it to the cross with His Son, Jesus Christ, who bore the weight of every sin. Our perfect, spotless Lamb atoned for the sins of the world, mine and yours included. We can run to the mercy seat and find grace, but we *must* run to the mercy seat to find grace. This grace is a restored, right relationship with God. This restored relationship will not be without temporal consequences for our sins, but they are His good discipline. We can receive whatever temporal consequences may come, knowing we will not face the eternal consequence for our sins because God forgave us.

The consequences of our sins may be painful, but God will work even those consequences for good for those who love Him, for those who have been called according to His purpose (Romans 8:28). Confessing our sins and repenting from them shows our heart's desire to obey God by turning from sin and trusting Him to keep His promise to forgive us and cleanse us from all unrighteousness (making us holy). We must come to a place of loving God and trusting Him more than loving our sin and trusting ourselves; this is the path toward holiness.

Sometimes we want to pursue holiness via a different avenue than God's. His path to holiness often requires suffering; sometimes, that suffering comes through consequences of our disobedience. We would much rather achieve holiness apart from that suffering; sometimes, we try to do that. The Pharisees who rejected Jesus took this approach. While they went through the motions of holy living, they didn't suffer grief over their sins because they denied committing any.

What Disobedience?

> "If we say we have not sinned, we make him a liar, and his word is not in us." 1 John 1:10

We can respond like David, confessing our sin, like Cain, becoming angry and remaining in our sin, or like the Pharisees, denying we have sinned at all. Even though Jesus Christ confronted them about their sins they continued to deny the accusations. They could not confess sin that they denied existed. Jesus proclaimed that He came to save the lost (Luke 19:10) and heal the sick (Mark 2:17). Many Pharisees did not think of themselves as lost in their sin or sick in their sin. People who don't think they are lost cannot be saved, and people who don't think they are sick do not seek a doctor for help. Those who don't think they have disobeyed God will not confess their disobedience. We cannot confess what we deny exists.

The Pharisees who rejected Jesus falsely believed they were keeping God's law. In a way, Cain thought the same. They went through the external motions of sacrifice and "obedience," but, unlike David, they did not sacrifice and obey from hearts of love and devotion to God. We battle this same struggle today. So many times, we try to obey God externally instead of from a heart of love and devotion to Him, possible only in the power of the Spirit. But this is what God wants to form in us—that beautiful heart of devotion to Him. It is because of this that He confronts our sin. His confrontation of our sin is not to condemn us in that sin but to free us from it.

We are not defined by our failures, but by how we respond to them. God is much more patient with us than we are with each other. Our culture wants to identify people by their mistakes and sins eternally, but God doesn't want to do that. He wants to identify His people by eternally forgiving their sins and changing them, conforming them to the image of His Son. Those He changes are the ones who rightly respond when confronted with their sins.

CHAPTER 25

Obedience with Sincerity

"For our boast is this, the testimony of our conscience, that we behaved in the world with simplicity and godly sincerity, not by earthly wisdom but by the grace of God, and supremely so toward you." 2 Corinthians 1:12

"Sincerity means that the appearance and the reality are exactly the same." Oswald Chambers[61]

We can all recall times of going through the motions but not feeling the connection between our inside attitude and our outside behavior. Others may not have noticed the disconnect, but we knew it was there. I battle this disconnect often, whether it's dinnertime and I have zero motivation to cook, or in more painful times when someone has hurt me deeply, and God calls me to respond in love. Though not always, I often say, "I want to want to!"

God commands us to obey Him, but we don't always want to act, speak, or think as He commands. We have a few options in these situations when our hearts don't want to obey. We can go through the right motions with the wrong heart and attitude (insincere "obedience"), we can choose not to do what we should because we don't want to (sincere disobedience), or we can admit our hearts are wrong and find help to do right (sincere obedience). The last option should be the aim of every Christian heart when we sense that disconnect between our desires and God's commands.

Looking at these options, how often do we fall into each of these categories? Too often we don't want to act, speak, or think rightly, so we

---

[61] Chambers, Oswald. 2008. *The Quotable Oswald Chambers.* Compiled by David McCasland. Discovery House.

either force it or avoid it, but God doesn't want either of those responses from us. He wants us to want to obey Him. This "wanting to want to" is no small thing. It reveals our heart's attitude toward God in our obedience. This desire to obey God is essential to sincere obedience.

Paul speaks of this sincerity frequently throughout the New Testament: In his first letter to the Corinthian church (1 Corinthians 5:8), many times in his second letter (2 Corinthians 1:12, 2 Corinthians 2:27, 2 Corinthians 8:8), in his letter to the Ephesian church (Ephesians 6:5), in his first letter to the Thessalonian church (1 Thessalonians 2:3-5), and in his first letter to Timothy (1 Timothy 1:5). Sincerity in the Church was a big deal to Paul because it was a big deal to God. Sincerity should be a big deal to us because it is a big deal to God.

Fighting Against Insincere "Obedience"

As I was studying for this chapter, I kept planning to go in another direction. I had a very short statement about sincerity regarding our obedience to God. But the more I read, meditated, and wrote, the more compelled I felt to speak to this issue of sincerity on a deeper level. I think insincerity has stunted the Church. We know we are to obey God's commands, but we have neglected the importance of obeying His commands with sincerity of heart. The world acts in opposition to God, but even Christians, more often than we want to admit, behave in ways that dishonor God, ways we may not even realize are displeasing to Him.

One of the greatest battles the Church is facing today is insincerity explained most simply as the disconnect between appearance and reality. Consider the following synonyms for insincerity: dishonesty, lying, falsehood, frivolousness, unimportance, untrustworthiness, and hollowness. When there is a disconnect between our actions and our heart, we are insincere because what appears is not reality. Jesus used the word hypocrisy.

Our Struggle with Legalism

"Not that we are sufficient in ourselves to claim anything as coming from us, but our sufficiency is from God, who has made us sufficient to be ministers of a new covenant, not of the letter

> but of the Spirit. For the letter kills, but the Spirit gives life."
> 2 Corinthians 3:5-6

Insincerity or hypocrisy are two words the Bible uses to describe this disconnect, but legalism is also a form of insincerity. Legalism obligates us to obey regardless of heart motive. It thinks, "If this is what the law says, then this is what I must do. If my heart doesn't agree with it, then I will act like it's true externally." Many Christians believe this is a right view of obedience to God, but it is a performance when we obey with the disconnect between our hearts and actions. It is hollow and insincere. It is obligation without willing submission.

Those who have grown up attending church have likely heard much talk about legalism and its dangers. But we haven't thought about its broad infestation nor how sneakily it creeps into all our lives. It's always a problem that "they" have, but we don't realize the struggle we have with it every day. Legalism is often our default response when we don't desire to do what God commands.

"But" you might argue, "God commands we keep His laws. What do we do when we don't want to obey? Isn't it better to do what He commands?" Legalism says, "Yes, it's better to do what God commands even if you don't want to." So, we do it because we are supposed to, not because we want to. But God warns us that the letter kills. It is the Spirit who gives life (2 Corinthians 3:6). We must ask ourselves, what is the power by which we perform this act of "obedience?" According to the letter, it kills or condemns us if we do it in the flesh. However, if we act in the Spirit, this is the obedience that gives life and pleases God. When we don't want to do what the Spirit prompts us to do, our hearts resist God's command. And if our heart is resisting, while we may act out the duty commanded, is that not contradictory to His command to love Him with all our heart, soul, mind, and strength? When we don't really want to obey in our hearts, we don't really want to obey. To "obey," in this case, would be dishonest.

Sincere Disobedience

> "Obedience to God is always possible. It is a deadly error to fall into the notion that when feelings are extremely strong, we can do nothing but act on them." Elisabeth Elliot[62]

---

[62] Elliot, Elisabeth. 2006. *Discipline: The Glad Surrender*. Revell.

Some may take this argument to the opposite extreme and say that if they don't desire to do something God commands, then they won't do it. Many decades of reacting against legalism have left us with a spirit of antinomianism—rejection of God's Law or even general rejection of laws and moral norms. Those who reject God do this by nature. Still, many people in churches have managed to spiritualize antinomianism by acting as though they are revering God in their effort to be transparent and true. They will site that their heart is not in it and, therefore, it would be disobedience anyway. Some may call it "authentic living," while others will reassure us of God's grace to receive us even when we "aren't feeling it." But this is a twisting of the truth. We are no less sinful by abstaining when we don't want to obey God's commands. We are committing the sin of omission by not doing what He commands us to do (James 4:17).

The outsider looking in on this discussion may say at this point, "Why in the world would you bother with this? It seems like a lose-lose situation." It does seem that way. If we do what God commands and our hearts are not motivated by the Spirit to willingly submit, it is disobedience masked in legalism. If we recognize our resistant, insubordinate hearts and choose not to do what God commands, we are still disobedient. Where do we go from here?

This is exactly where we need to be for God to take us to sincere obedience. We need to recognize the flesh's tendency toward insincere "obedience" or sincere disobedience. Left to our own strength and power, we cannot obey God with sincerity because we will never desire to obey Him. Jesus Christ, through the power of the Spirit, is our only hope for sincere obedience to God.

Sincere obedience begins with acknowledging our need for God's help to obey sincerely. The Spirit makes us willing to obey. The Spirit enters our disobedience, stubbornness, and unbelief and gives us the desire to obey God. Any desire to obey God is not from us but from His Spirit. The Spirit of God gives us what we would not have apart from Him—the desire to please God. With this godly sincerity comes honesty, gravity, and meaning. We understand the weightiness of our calling, not taking it, or Him, lightly. Through this sincere obedience, we find our life's meaning and purpose as we love and obey Him.

Sincere Obedience and the Fear of the Lord

> "Bondservants, obey in everything those who are your earthly masters, not by way of eye-service, as people-pleasers, but with sincerity of heart, fearing the Lord." Colossians 3:22

Sincere obedience is rooted in the fear of the Lord. It is not deceptive, frivolous, forced, or hollow but honest, weighty, willing, and Spirit-filled. It always looks upward, beyond the circumstances. It is God-focused. Paul makes this point when he tells the enslaved Christians in Colossae to obey their masters, not to please men, but to please God. He exhorted the Ephesians to the same high standard of obedience as he called wives to submit to their husbands, husbands to love their wives, children to obey their parents and honor them, and again to the enslaved Christians, he said this: "Bondservants, obey your earthly masters with fear and trembling, with a sincere heart, as you would Christ, not by way of eye-service, as people-pleasers, but as bondservants of Christ, do the will of God from the heart, rendering service with a good will as to the Lord and not to man" (Ephesians 6:5-7). Paul wanted them, and us, to understand that our actions are not merely an external submission to one another within a family, business, church, or country; they should flow from an internal, willing submission to God.

Obedience, as God intends, is first an act of the heart. God knows the motives of our hearts anyway, so to act "by way of eye-service," aiming to impress the people around us, does not persuade Him. When we live in God-focused fear, we honor and revere Him not just when people are looking but when people are not. We obey Him not just when people can look but when they can't. Our obedience must be rooted in the truth that God is our witness (Philippians 1:8) and He is looking at our hearts (1 Samuel 16:7).

Christ's Heart and Our Sincerity

> "For our appeal does not spring from error or impurity or any attempt to deceive, but just as we have been approved by God to be entrusted with the gospel, so we speak, not to please man, but to please God who tests our hearts. For we never came with words of flattery, as you know, nor a pretext for greed—God is witness. Nor did we seek glory from people…" 1 Thessalonians 2:3-6

We cannot obey God with sincerity of heart if our hearts are sinful by nature. As the gospel always does, this speaks to our need for Christ's intervention in our lives—not just once but constantly. It is not a heart driven by the sinful flesh that obeys God with sincerity but a new heart, given us by God when we believe. And this heart has only one mode of obedience: sincerity. The challenge for us on this side of glory is to remain yielded to the desires of our new heart, refusing to revert to the old ways of the fleshly heart (1 Peter 1:14). When we sense that temptation, which we naturally do, this is when we cry out: "I want to want to! Lord, help me." This is similar to what the father cried out when Jesus told him anything was possible to those who believe: "I believe; help my unbelief" (Mark 9:24). In this place of willing submission, the Spirit changes our desires, fills our faithlessness with faithfulness, and helps us live sincere lives of obedience by grace through faith for the glory of God.

CHAPTER 26

The Fruit of Faith

"You did not choose me, but I chose you and appointed you so that you might go and bear fruit—fruit that will last..." John 15:16 (NIV)

"We must come to good works by faith, and not to faith by good works." William Gurnall[63]

Obedience is the fruit of faith. Too often, we neglect faith's role in our obedience. We don't see them working together but as separate entities thinking, "My faith in Jesus Christ is one thing, but my obedience to Him is another, different thing." But obedience that pleases God comes from faith. This faith-filled obedience is a gift from God. It is a work of grace by the Spirit as He gives us both the desire and power to act. The faith God gives His people will always come with identifiable marks. We identify God-fearing people by their faith in God and their faith in God can be identified by how they live.

Just as you recognize a banana tree because it produces bananas, you know those who have faith in Jesus Christ by their obedience to Him. God-fearing obedience is sincere, but it is also evident. The Bible calls this evident obedience "good works" or fruit. It is visible evidence of an invisible, internal reality: our faith.

Faith in Every Good Work

> "...walk in a manner worthy of the Lord, to please Him in all respects, bearing fruit in every good work and increasing in the knowledge of God;" Colossians 1:10

---

[63] Gurnall, William. 2008. *Extracts from the Writings of William Gurnall*. Scripture Truth.

Without faith, it is impossible to please God (Hebrews 11:6). That means faith doesn't just occur at justification (when we first believe) but goes beyond our justification (as we continue believing). We can't just say we have faith and live how we want to live if that way of life contradicts God's commands. That is not faith but disobedience.

Faith is more than a trophy we receive at a single point in time. Faith is not just something we have but how we live. When we have faith in Jesus Christ, the indwelling Holy Spirit equips us with the power to please God. We demonstrate our faith every time we yield to the Spirit's work in our lives. Faith is the root of every good work. Everything we do that pleases God is done by faith. There is no good work done apart from faith because faith is the fuel that makes our work pleasing to God. We can say we have faith but until we demonstrate that faith by obedience (good works), then that faith is meaningless. It is dead. I think this is what Paul means when he says that we have been saved *through* faith.

Faith and Works

> "For by grace you have been saved through faith. And this is not your own doing; it is the gift of God, not a result of works, so that no one may boast. For we are his workmanship, created in Christ Jesus for good works, which God prepared beforehand, that we should walk in them." Ephesians 2:8-10

The Bible teaches us the right relationship between faith and works, yet the debate continues about the role of works in our faith. The disagreement usually stems from confusion regarding the word "works." Paul writes that it is by grace through faith... not a result of works, that we gain salvation (Ephesians 2:8-9). James writes that faith, apart from works, is dead (James 2:26). These are the two passages that most often come to the forefront in this discussion. It appears Paul and James contradict themselves, but we need to remember that Ephesians 2:10 says: "For we are His workmanship, created in Christ Jesus for good works, which God prepared beforehand that we should walk in them." James doesn't contradict Paul but agrees with him.

To understand their agreement, we must understand the difference between the two works Paul refers to in Ephesians 2:8-10. "Works" in verse 9 speaks of our works in the flesh (disobedience), while "good works" in verse 10 speaks of works done in the Spirit (obedience). The latter "good works" are the ones that prove our faith and please God. Those "good works" show we fear God because they bring Him glory while the former "works" aim to bring us glory. The latter "good works" are the ones that James says show our faith is genuine. Good works are evidence of God's work in us. The works that prove our faith are never in our own power and never seek to bring ourselves glory. They are always in the Spirit's power for the glory of God.

Visible Faith

> "Now faith is the substance of things hoped for, the evidence of things not seen." Hebrews 11:1 (NKJV)

Hebrews 11 focuses on specific men and women of faith. None of these men and women possessed a blind, lazy, unidentifiable faith, but their obedience was what the writer of Hebrews used to validate their faith. Instead of the Hall of Faith, we could call it the Hall of Obedience—not to say obedience replaces faith, but to emphasize obedience is the fruit of faith.

Believing God cannot be separated from doing what He says. We know this by Abraham's example. He obeyed God by leaving his home when called to go to the land of his inheritance (Hebrews 11:8). The Bible also tells us it was by faith that Abraham "when he was tested, offered up Isaac" (Hebrews 11:17). He believed God and trusted Him to keep His promises even if that meant God raised Isaac from the dead. He had faith to believe God could raise Isaac to keep His word.

In Genesis 22, when God calls Abraham to sacrifice Isaac, Abraham's faith is made evident by his obedience. As he lifts the knife to slay his son, the angel of the LORD says to him, "Do not lay your hand on the boy or do anything to him, for now I know that you fear God, seeing you have not withheld your son, your only son, from me" (Genesis 22:12). We should not miss the fact that it was by Abraham's actions that the angel of the LORD declared that Abraham feared God.

Abraham proved that he feared God not by saying he did but by doing what God asked of him. And it was no small request. He was willing to obey even if that meant giving up the child God promised him, the child he loved dearly and through whom God promised to bless all the nations of the world. Everything from Abraham's perspective, all God's promised blessings to him, hinged on his son, Isaac. But God had proven Himself faithful to Abraham many times before. God stretched Abraham's faith during the years he walked with Him. Abraham learned to trust God even when it didn't make sense, obey Him even if it was costly, and do what He said even if it seemed like he was giving everything up. God calls *us* to live this way. Not with passive faith but active, evident, and often costly obedience by faith.

Costly Fruit

> "Words are cheap. It is by costly, self-denying Christian practice that we show the reality of our faith." Jonathan Edwards[64]

"Unless a grain of wheat falls into the earth and dies, it remains alone; but if it dies, it bears much fruit" (John 12:24). For the fruit of faith to flourish, we must die to everything else. Looking back over the list of men and women of faith in Hebrews 11, we see their works of faith were acts of costly obedience. They risked much to obey God. Their willingness to sacrifice anything to obey God proved their faith was real. They all had a common theme in their faith: complete surrender to God's will. Abraham and Isaac demonstrated this complete surrender no matter the cost, foreshadowing the perfect example of ultimate surrender to God's will in the life of Jesus Christ. No one risked more or gave up more than Jesus, who "though he was in the form of God, did not count equality with God a thing to be grasped, but emptied himself, by taking the form of a servant, being born in the likeness of men. And being found in human form, he humbled himself by becoming obedient to the point of death, even death on a cross" (Philippians 2:6-8).

In *The Cost of Discipleship,* Dietrich Bonhoeffer explains the connection between faith and works and how they show a fully surrendered life to God, no matter the cost. He contrasted the cost of discipleship with this idea of cheap grace that we have confused with faith. He describes cheap grace as faith without a cost—we get to believe what we want to believe, do what we want to do, live the way we want to live, and never really have to give up our dreams, desires, and, most importantly, our sin; this is truly the self-focused life. It is the antithesis of a God-focused and God-fearing life. It puts us, fallen humans, in a place of authority as we assert for ourselves what and how we will obey God. If we judge it too costly, then we can choose not to act on that command and excuse ourselves from that which demands too much of us. But Jesus told us clearly: "If anyone would come after me, let him deny himself and take up his cross and follow me.

---

[64] Edwards, Jonathan. 2016. *The Experience that Counts.* Christian Heritage.

For whoever would save his life will lose it, but whoever loses his life for my sake will find it" (Matthew 16:24-25). The point of our lives is not to avoid suffering; the cost of discipleship is great. We must consider that as we progress in our relationship with Jesus Christ and watch how the Lord keeps His promise that when we lose our lives for His sake, we actually find them.

The life of faith in Christ is not easy, but it is rewarding. It is the only path to life. We may lose our lives literally or in the sense that we give up our fleshly desires, but we will find the lives God meant for us to have—abundant, fruitful, and forever glorious. "For you have died, and your life is hidden with Christ in God. When Christ who is your life appears, then you also will appear with him in glory" (Colossians 3:2-3).

Our Obedience and God's Glory

> "So, whether you eat or drink, or whatever you do, do all to the glory of God." 1 Corinthians 10:31

There is no greater purpose for our obedience to God than His glory. Our entire lives are meant to glorify God, as Scripture teaches and the Westminster Catechism famously affirms. And our obedience is a necessary part of that formula. Fearing God and obeying Him is how we can accomplish our chief end. There is no way to glorify God apart from obedience to His commands, and there is no way to enjoy Him forever apart from obedience to His commandments (Matthew 7:21-23).

As Jesus commissioned His disciples before His ascension, He called them to obedience in action: "And Jesus came and said to them, 'All authority in heaven and on earth has been given to me. Go therefore and make disciples of all nations, baptizing them in the name of the Father and of the Son and of the Holy Spirit, teaching them to observe all that I have commanded you. And behold, I am with you always, to the end of the age'" (Matthew 28:18-20). We glorify God by obeying Him and teaching others to do the same. This is not an abstract "glorify God" but an identifiable and observable "glorify God" by faith, as we fear God and keep His commandments. It is a glorification that manifests itself in our obedience. "Manifest" means to make visible the invisible, which is what our lives do when we fear God and obey Him—we manifest His glory as His Spirit, who is with us always, empowers us to do His will. We glorify God by fearing Him and keeping His commandments, the fruit of our faith.

PART VI
Suffering and the Fear of God

CHAPTER 27

Revealing Fears

"For I consider that the sufferings of this present time are not worth comparing with the glory that is to be revealed to us." Romans 8:18

"We only know ourselves and what we really are when the force of circumstances brings us out." Elizabeth Prentiss[65]

Suffering is universal. No one escapes it. It's one of the few things in life we all wish would go away. Even Christians struggle to understand God's mysterious ways regarding our suffering. But as long as we are on this earth, we will face it.

The Bible teaches us a great deal about suffering. People get the wrong idea that Christianity should be free of suffering, or at least the appearance of suffering. That is not a biblical understanding of Christianity. God's Word promises that we will have tribulations (John 16:33) and that the afflictions of the righteous are many (Psalm 34:19). Remember that all who desire to live a godly life in Christ Jesus will experience persecution (2 Timothy 3:12), that we will suffer for the sake of Christ (Philippians 1:29), and that we will share in His sufferings (Philippians 3:10, 1 Peter 4:12-19). Christianity without suffering is not Christianity.

There is a guarantee of suffering in this world, but it is not pointless. Consider what Scripture tells us about suffering. Our suffering produces endurance which leads to character that produces hope (Romans 5:3-4), and our suffering cannot separate us from the love of Christ (Romans 8:35). We

---

[65] Prentiss, Elizabeth. 1998. *Stepping Heavenward: One Woman's Journey to Godliness.* Barbour.

are not alone in our suffering; God will comfort us in all our affliction (2 Corinthians 1:3) and, in turn, His comfort in our affliction will equip us to comfort others in theirs (2 Corinthians 1:4). Our suffering is not without purpose: when we suffer for righteousness' sake, we will be blessed (1 Peter 3:14) and our affliction is preparing for us an eternal weight of glory (2 Corinthians 4:17). Ultimately, our suffering is not permanent because we have the promise of being delivered out of all our afflictions (Psalm 34:19) and one day it will all be over, and all our suffering will end forever (Revelation 21:1-5). It is important to distinguish that these promises of suffering and promises for good to come from that suffering are not for all people but "for those who love God... who are called according to His purpose" (Romans 8:28). These promises are for those who fear God.

Suffering and the Fear of God

> "By affliction He teaches us many precious lessons, which without it we should never learn. By affliction He shows us our emptiness and weakness, draws us to the throne of grace, purifies our affections, weans us from the world, makes us long for heaven." J. C. Ryle[66]

We don't often connect our suffering with the fear of the LORD. Suffering is a unique subcategory for fearing God because it isn't exactly like wisdom, love, and obedience. These are manifestations of the fear of God in the Christian's life, but our wisdom, love, and obedience are often revealed, tested, and matured through our suffering. In other words, suffering is the condition in which God tests our fear of Him and makes our holiness more complete (James 1:2-4).

While suffering is universal, how we handle it is not. There might be an endless list of ways we deal with our suffering, but each of those will ultimately filter down to two ways: we either turn to God or turn away from Him. Suffering itself doesn't cause people to turn to God or cause them to turn from Him. Instead, it reveals the inner state of our souls. Suffering exposes our hearts. Some may be drawn to God in their suffering, while others may push Him away. The fear of the LORD determines whether a person turns to or away from God in their suffering.

---

[66] Ryle, J. C. 2015. *Bible Commentary- Gospel of Mark*. Editora Dracaena.

In chapter six, "The Right Fear Among Wrong Fears," we learned about two fears found in Scripture: self-focused fear and God-focused fear. Everything we think, say, and do stems from one of these two fears. Self-focused fear is sin, while God-focused fear pleases God. No matter our circumstances, we can think, speak and act in self-focused fear or God-focused fear depending on whether we are led by our flesh or the Spirit. Our flesh always responds with a hard heart of self-focused fear, while the Spirit always responds in God-focused fear.

In relation to our suffering, those who fear the LORD will turn to Him and trust Him by faith. Those who do not fear the LORD will respond in self-focused fear, looking everywhere for help but God. We can conclude that only those who fear the LORD are drawn to Him in their suffering because our natural inclination is to blame God. In our flesh, we hate our suffering and hate that in His sovereignty, He would allow it. Our flesh wants to deny and avoid suffering, while the Spirit empowers us to face it with joy, knowing God has ordained it in His providence for our good and His glory. Only a work of grace in the heart could do something as significant as drawing us toward God in worship and adoration, even and especially in our suffering.

God allows suffering for various reasons. On this side of heaven, we will wonder what many of them are, but some reasons we can know clearly. God allows suffering to test our fear of Him, to rid us of our self-focused fear, and to graciously give us eyes to see Him, the source and subject of our holy fear, more clearly.

To Test Our Fear

> "In this you rejoice, though now for a little while, if necessary, you have been grieved by various trials, so that the tested genuineness of your faith—more precious than gold that perishes though it is tested by fire—may be found to result in praise and glory and honor at the revelation of Jesus Christ."
> 1 Peter 1:6-7

Suffering tests the reality of our faith and exposes the state of our hearts. God ordains our suffering, but He doesn't use our suffering to tempt us. God tempts no one (James 1:13-15). God never lures us into self-focused fear (sin).

The flesh and the devil do that. For those who are led by the Spirit of God, our suffering will reveal the fear of the LORD driving our hearts. This is reflected over and over in the lives of God's people, both those highlighted on the pages of Scripture, and those who surround us today.

To Purge Self-Focused Fear

> "It is good for me that I was afflicted, that I might learn your statutes." Psalm 119:71

Those who fear the LORD grieve their sin because their new hearts desire to be holy as God is holy (1 Peter 1:15). They want to turn from their sin and turn to God. It is often in their suffering that God exposes their sins, stripping them of whatever they love more or depend on more than Himself. God uses our suffering to free us from our bondage to sin so we can see Him more clearly, turn in the right direction (away from sin and toward God), and seek His help to live a life of joyful obedience. Through our suffering, God purges us of self-focused fear, filling those spaces with God-focused fear that leads us to holiness "without which no one can see the Lord" (Hebrews 12:14). His beauty and holiness shine before us with such glory and majesty we can't help but bow our lives in praise to Him.

To Reveal Fear Himself

> "Beloved, do not be surprised at the fiery trial when it comes upon you to test you, as though something strange were happening to you. But rejoice insofar as you share Christ's sufferings, that you may also rejoice and be glad when his glory is revealed." 1 Peter 4:12-13

God's glory is not separate from Himself; it is the manifestation of His character. Suffering is the darkest backdrop for a reason. It magnifies the brightest and most beautiful Star of the show. When we fear God in our suffering, He reveals Himself to us personally, and to those around us as His Spirit glorifies Himself. The trials and tribulations of life are opportunities to witness God's power and glory not only in our circumstances but through His work in our own hearts. We witness His Spirit move us from hopelessness to hope, grief to joy, and pain to peace. We witness this good work because of God's mercy and grace, not only in our current suffering but because of the greatest suffering. Through His suffering, Jesus Christ made a way for us to see and know God.

The Greatest Suffering for the Greatest Reason

> "For there is no distinction: for all have sinned and fall short of the glory of God, and are justified by his grace as a gift, through the redemption that is in Christ Jesus, whom God put forward as a propitiation by his blood, to be received by faith." Romans 3:22-25

The greatest suffering was the means through which God offered humanity the greatest gift: our salvation. God demonstrated His loving purpose for suffering: to save sinners through Jesus Christ's willing submission to the Father's will, even to the point of death on a cross. In Christ's death and resurrection, God offers a way to redeem our lives and circumstances. The pathway to that beautiful redemption was unimaginable suffering.

When we believe in Christ's atoning work on the cross, His Spirit gives us the same power to overcome sin and death, "For we do not have a high priest who is unable to sympathize with our weaknesses, but one who in every respect has been tempted as we are, yet without sin" (Hebrews 4:15). The sinless High Priest is our Mediator. Because of Christ, we can live clothed with His undeserved righteousness, which grants us eternal access to God and communion with Him, even in our suffering. But just as Jesus willingly submitted to the Father in His suffering, trusting God would glorify Himself through it, so, too, must we decide to submit our lives to the Father, trusting He will glorify Himself through our suffering.

Our Choice in Suffering

A few years ago, I came across a quote that said, "If you feel far from God, guess who moved?"[67] What a poignant statement. God calls us to come to Him and so often, when we stubbornly walk in the opposite direction or ignorantly drift away from Him, He uses suffering to draw us back to Himself. If we draw near to Him, He promises to draw near to us (James 4:8).

---

[67] Gunn, Robin J. 1990. *Surprise Endings*. Bethany House.

But we don't always turn to God in our suffering. Sometimes we may turn to Him, but other times we may push Him away. We have all fallen short, and our flesh constantly hinders us from that perfect communion with God. So, this truth, those who turn to God fear Him and those who turn away from Him don't, is not defined in isolation, based on one trial. We need not ever think we missed our chance to turn to God. "The Lord is merciful and gracious, slow to anger and abounding in steadfast love" (Psalm 103:8). He longs to be gracious to us when we repent of our self-reliance or rebellion and turn to Him (Isaiah 30:18).

With each trial and test, we have a choice in our suffering. We can turn away from God in anger and frustration and strive in vain to restore the brokenness around us and in us, or we can turn to God in holy fear and reverence and say, with all our hearts, "The Lord gives, and the Lord takes away, blessed be the name of the Lord" (Job 1:21).

When we turn to God in our suffering, it is not some pie-in-the-sky, automatic resolution to our pain nor a robotic suppression of our grief. As we read in the account of Job's suffering, as only one example, fearing the Lord in our turning to Him is not a mechanical act but a passionate one that confesses our helplessness and hopelessness apart from Him. It is a holy call for Him to do what we cannot do—turn our mourning to dancing and our pain into good purpose, creating beauty from ashes. And He will do it.

CHAPTER 28

The Significance of Trust

"You who fear the LORD, trust in the LORD! He is their help and their shield." Psalm 115:11

"Trusting God means thinking and acting according to God's word in spite of circumstances, feelings, or consequences." Warren Wiersbe[68]

How can you know you trust someone until you need to? In C. S. Lewis's book, *A Grief Observed*, he journaled about his suffering after the death of his wife. He wrote of his doubts and fears, how he wrestled with God and struggled to trust Him at times. In his suffering, he discovered profound truths about trusting God. Early in the book he writes,

> You never know how much you really believe anything until its truth or falsehood becomes a matter of life and death to you. It is easy to say you believe a rope to be strong and sound as long as you are merely using it to cord a box. But suppose you had to hang by that rope over a precipice. Wouldn't you then first discover how much you really trusted it?[69]

The reality of our trust, or faith, in God is never clearer than in our suffering because it is in these points of testing that we discover the authenticity of our claims. In any matter of trust, if our claims are true, then we will trust at that most dangerous and reckless point, and we will discover the trustworthiness,

---

[68] Wiersbe, Warren W. 1996. *Being a Child of God: Your Guide for the Adventure.* Thomas Nelson Publishers.
[69] Lewis, C. S. 2001. *A Grief Observed.* HarperOne.

or not, of whatever it was that we trusted. But if we claim to trust, yet at the most dangerous and reckless point turn back or take matters into our own hands, we will never know whether whatever it was that we "trusted" before was trustworthy. Lewis writes, "I thought I trusted the rope until it mattered to me whether it would bear me. Now it matters, and I find I didn't." The significance of trust—its meaningfulness and authenticity—directly correlates with our suffering. We do not know the importance or reality of our trust in God until that trust is tested in our suffering.

Understanding Trust

Trusting God is not a setting Christians are programmed to have at all times. We have the ever-present ability to trust God through His Spirit within us, but our default will be self-reliance unless we yield to Him. Trusting God is an active choice, a choice we will have to make over and over again. It is not merely a verbal confession but a visual conviction that moves us voluntarily in the direction God moves us, often into dangerous and scary places. The choice to follow God into these places is not a blind trust but one that we base on His faithfulness. The evidence of His faithfulness in the past helps us trust Him in the present. As we trust God and believe He loves us and always keeps His promises to us, even when the circumstances may try to tell us otherwise, we find Him faithful and trustworthy. Our lives become never-ending wheels that move from suffering to trust to growing faith back to suffering, and so on. The wheel cannot rotate forward if one of these is not engaged, but God is sovereign and faithfully moves us around the wheel that propels us forward as He ordains our suffering, equips us to trust Him, and matures our faith through it all.

There are numerous examples in Scripture of God's work to build His people's trust in suffering, but we will look at just two, one from the Old Testament and one from the New Testament. In both stories, they struggled to trust God, something to which we can all relate. But God had no plans to forsake them in their struggle. He used their suffering as a platform to reveal Himself in powerful ways—saving them, helping them, and moving them closer to Himself with a deeper and more abiding trust in Him, based on His love and faithfulness that they experienced personally. These stories remind us that God's faithfulness is not dependent on our behavior but on His character.

They prove that the LORD is moving us around the wheel as He gives us eyes to see and hearts to believe that God is faithful and worthy of our trust.

When We Trust

> "And when the Israelites saw the mighty hand of the LORD displayed against the Egyptians, the people feared the LORD and put their trust in him and in Moses his servant." Exodus 14:31 (NIV)

One of the most incredible stories of God's power displayed for the salvation of His people is the parting of the Red Sea. When the Israelites realized the massive Egyptian army was after them as they escaped Egypt, "they feared greatly" (Exodus 14:10). They cried out to the LORD while complaining to Moses that he brought them there to die, facing a sea before them and an army behind them. Their self-focused fear overwhelmed them, but Moses responded, "Fear not, stand firm, and see the salvation of the LORD, which he will work for you today" (Exodus 14:13). As the Israelites trembled with self-focused fear, sure of their impending doom, God had good plans to help them—not easy plans, but good plans. The LORD commanded Moses to tell the people of Israel to go forward, and God displayed His power by parting the sea, making a way where there seemed to be no way.

We read this passage and speak with understandable awe and excitement that God saved them so miraculously, but we usually stop at the parting of the sea. We don't consider that the Israelites had to choose to walk through the sea, with walls of water on either side. He parted the sea for them, but they had to take the steps across the dry land. The miraculous work itself didn't save them from the Egyptians. They had to decide if they were going to walk through it. They had to trust that God loved and cared for them and would love and care for them as they walked with high walls of water on either side of them with nothing holding the mighty waters back but the Word of God. Scripture tells us twice, "the people of Israel walked on dry ground through the sea, the waters being a wall to them on their right hand and on their left" (Exodus 14:22, 29).

As I try to imagine the scene, the emotions they may have experienced are terror, awe, and fear. Certainly, the Israelites were shocked by how God planned to save them. I don't think there were happy celebrators so much as reverent worshipers as they witnessed His power and walked forward in God-focused fear and trust. But even as they walked forward, their suffering wasn't over. They had hours to walk through the sea. Every step they took was a conscientious confession of trust. God doesn't teleport us out of our suffering because our journey out is an important part of His work. He is building our faith as we choose to trust Him for help. In many ways, the journey out of suffering is part of the suffering. The way out is not easy because it requires that we give up our own efforts and surrender to a powerful God, trusting Him completely as we realize the impossibility of saving ourselves. This process can sometimes be more difficult or painful than the suffering we faced before, but the results of that trust and surrender will far outweigh the struggle at the start. God will show Himself faithful.

When We Don't

> "The steadfast love of the LORD never ceases, his mercies never come to an end; they are new every morning; great is your faithfulness." Lamentations 3:22-23

Though at times we fail to trust God, He still proves He is trustworthy because He remains faithful to us. The disciples experienced many trials that tested their trust in Jesus. They were not merely acquainted with Jesus but those closest to Him. They saw His miracles, experienced His patience, and received His loving kindness countless times. Still, they failed to love and fear Him faithfully. One particular trial happened soon after Jesus called them. They were together on a boat facing a terrifying storm. As the scene plays out, we see what we always see when our trust in God fails: our faithlessness juxtaposed with Christ's faithfulness.

> And a great windstorm arose, and the waves were breaking into the boat, so that the boat was already filling. But he was in the stern, asleep on the cushion. And they woke him and said to him, "Teacher, do you not care that we are perishing?" And he awoke and rebuked the wind and said to the sea, "Peace! Be still!" And the wind ceased, and there was a great calm. He said to them, "Why are you so afraid? Have you still no faith?" And they were filled with great fear and said to one another,

"Who then is this, that even the wind and the sea obey him?"
Mark 4:37-41

The disciples faced a raging storm while Jesus slept on a cushion in the stern. They woke Him convinced that He didn't care as they prepared to die, a similar response to the Israelites at the Red Sea. The following seconds shifted their fear as Jesus awoke and commanded the wind to stop and the sea to be still. They witnessed the glory of God in the person of Jesus Christ and responded in the only right way—filled with great fear.

Jesus exposed their self-focused fears, rooting that fear back to a lack of faith. Yet in their faithlessness, God remained faithful; He could not deny His own character (2 Timothy 2:13). Their faith failed, but God did not. Witnessing His faithfulness on full display reoriented their fear.

Similar examples happen over and over throughout Scripture as bad things happen and people suffer. Some doubt God's goodness and assume He doesn't care about them. Their faith falters just like the disciples on the boat. In John 11, we read that Jesus knew Lazarus was sick; yet he waited and intentionally arrived after Lazarus had died. To his family and friends, it may have looked like Jesus didn't care; but when Jesus heard Lazarus was sick, his first response was this: "This illness does not lead to death. It is for the glory of God, so that the Son of God may be glorified through it" (John 11:4). That was exactly what happened. Jesus raised Lazarus from the dead and glorified God.

When God allows His people to suffer, it is because it will be the perfect platform to display His glory and increase their faith. Had God prevented the storm that terrified the disciples, they would not have witnessed His power and sovereign control over creation. Had Jesus arrived in time to heal Lazarus, the people would not have witnessed His power to raise the dead. Had God not allowed a particular trial in our lives, we would not be able to reflect on that time and recall His faithfulness. When God's people experience His faithfulness, they grow in fear and faith; therefore, Christians need not grieve without hope in their suffering. He will prove Himself trustworthy as we wait on Him, trusting His good plan.

Our Trustworthy Anchor

> "In order to realize the worth of the anchor, we need to feel the stress of the storm." Corrie Ten Boom[70]

Similar to Lewis's illustration of trusting the rope, Corrie Ten Boom reminds us that until we experience the stress of the storm, we cannot recognize the value and worth of the anchor. The storms are opportunities to prove the anchor's value in the same way our suffering is an opportunity to prove God's trustworthiness. So, paradoxically, the storms of life are not great disasters but a life without storms. Through our suffering, we grow in our dependence on the LORD. The tragedy is not living through many storms and trials but living without an anchor to help us withstand them. How precious is the trustworthy Anchor that has proven He can withstand all the storms, one hit after another. And how sweet are the storms that remind us of the worth of our Anchor and prove His worth to the world.

---

[70] Boom, Corrie T. 1985. *Jesus Is Victor.* Fleming H. Revell Company.

CHAPTER 29

The Good Gift of Suffering

"And we know that for those who love God all things work together for good, for those who are called according to his purpose. For those whom he foreknew he also predestined to be conformed to the image of his Son, in order that he might be the firstborn among many brothers." Romans 8:28-29

"I suggest to you that it is because God loves us that he gives us the gift of suffering. Pain is God's megaphone to rouse a deaf world. You see, we are like blocks of stone out of which the Sculptor carves the forms of men. The blows of his chisel, which hurt us so much are what make us perfect." C.S. Lewis[71]

I remember getting the call from my doctor's office after dropping my daughter off at preschool. My husband and I had two previous miscarriages and the doctors closely monitored this third baby in these early weeks. The blood test results showed the pregnancy hormone going down, so they wanted me to come in. As I continued the drive home, I remember banging on the steering wheel with tears welling up in my eyes. I cried out to God, "You give good gifts. This baby is good. Please don't take this baby!" I quoted Scripture related to God's goodness and grace. I felt like Abraham, Moses, and so many others when they spoke with God, pleading for Him to be merciful (Genesis 18:22-33, Exodus 32:11-14). They spoke of His character and His promises. Their "talking back" to God was their confession of faith in Him, pleading with Him to keep His Word. I was begging, too, and basing my plea on God's character. We lost that sweet baby.

I didn't understand God's ways. It was one of the hardest seasons of

---

[71] Lewis, C. S. 2015. *The Problem of Pain*. HarperOne.

my life. Looking back, I realized that I was trying to define God and His ways from my perspective, as we can so easily do when we lean on our own understanding. "God, your goodness looks like this." "God, your love and faithfulness look like this." In asking the LORD to save my baby, I was trying to reconcile my definition of "good things" with God's perfect and complete understanding of "good things." I had not considered the trials of our miscarriages as the good God had in mind. I don't say this flippantly, but with the gravity and weight it deserves. When I say the trial was the good God intended, I mean He had a good purpose in my suffering. It was not in vain. I just needed His perspective to see that.

Perspective in Suffering

> "Every good gift and every perfect gift is from above, coming down from the Father of lights, with whom there is no variation or shadow due to change." James 1:17

James opens his letter to the dispersed church with encouragement regarding the testing of their faith. The first several verses in the passage are more familiar to us than the last few. I had never really considered the placement of James 1:17, speaking of every good and perfect gift coming from God. I always thought that verse referred to "good gifts" and "perfect gifts" that we would all agree are good, like babies and blessings that we want. But it is one of the last verses James writes in the passage about the testing of our faith, an important context for us to consider.

The verse directly preceding it, verse 16, warns us, "Do not be deceived, my beloved brothers." It seems misplaced, as though it should end the previous paragraph about our fleshly desires luring us and enticing us to sin. But it doesn't end that paragraph. It starts the new one. And following that verse, he talks about these good and perfect gifts. Together these verses seem oddly placed, but when we read the passage in its entirety, we must ask, "What do these verses have to do with the testing of our faith?" Could James be warning the Church not to be deceived by our own perceptions of good gifts?

From our fleshly perspective, we will only consider the gifts we want to be good. But if that is our only perspective, we are likely missing many good gifts that we label as bad ones. James is warning us not to mislabel God's good gifts. He is our loving Father who has no malicious intent but means to do good for His children. Not good as in, "I'll let you eat cookies for breakfast every day," but good as in, "I know what is best for you." He is love and goodness, so everything that comes from His hand to His children is intended for their good because He loves them, even if that includes suffering (Genesis 50:20). The good gifts James speaks of are not from our perspective but from God's.

Reading the previous chapter, you may have thought, "But I did trust God and He wasn't faithful, He wasn't good, He wasn't loving, and things went badly." I have had those same thoughts. However, when we think this way, are we not defining God's character from our perspective and our assessment of the situation? Are we not concluding that God's faithfulness means that He does things as we think He should? But who are we to know the ways of God? We are on His timeline; He is not on ours. We cannot presume that trial or its purposes are complete. Yes, it may be in the past, but God can still redeem it in the present or the future.

If we are willing to ask for God's perspective, He will show it to us. He will help us see the good in the suffering we face. God has graciously shown my husband and me some good from that painful trial of our miscarriages. Practically, there was the discovery of health issues I had that needed addressing. Doctors found these issues as we sought explanations for our miscarriages. Personally, the Lord has softened both my husband and I toward others who have experienced loss, whether through miscarriage or otherwise. Just as He comforted us through His Word and Spirit, especially through His people who loved us well, we became better equipped to comfort others (2 Corinthians 1:3-4). We are more sensitive and sympathetic to the pain of those around us, which would not have been possible without the tremendous pain we experienced ourselves. This second point is true for us not just through our miscarriages but also regarding the other trials we have faced individually and as a couple. Each trial has uniquely changed us. We are not the same people we were before, and that is by God's good design.

Progress in Suffering

> "Count it all joy, my brothers, when you meet trials of various kinds, for you know that the testing of your faith produces steadfastness. And let steadfastness have its full effect, that you may be perfect and complete, lacking in nothing." James 1:2-4

Through our trials, God is transforming us into the image of Christ; this is sanctification, the process of growing in holiness. We know sanctification is progressive, but we usually think of that progress strictly on a timeline—we change from year to year, decade to decade. While this is true, we can also view our sanctification in the "well-rounded" aspect. If we think of sanctification like a puzzle, God is putting the pieces of our lives together. He promises to continue working on us until we are finished or complete (Philippians 1:6). He will put every piece in place, and in the end, we will look like Jesus. Until every piece is in place, however, we are incomplete.

When reading the first few verses in James, I always brushed over the phrase "of various kinds," focusing on trials in general testing our faith to produce steadfastness. It wasn't until I reflected on some of the greatest moments that tested my faith, each very different, that the Lord impressed upon me the significance of the phrase "of various kinds." I have faced a variety of challenges, struggles, and trials, as I'm sure you have. It's a mixed bag. Each trial has been unique, even if they may be in the same category (relational, ministerial, personal, etc.) The variety of our trials is no accident. Just like each puzzle piece is different yet necessary for the completed picture, each trial we face is unique but important to complete God's work in us. Through our "various trials" that produce steadfastness, God is working to finish the puzzle of our lives, so we will be "perfect and complete, lacking in nothing."

The writer of Hebrews tells us, "[We] do not have a high priest who is unable to sympathize with our weaknesses, but one who in every respect has been tempted as we are, yet without sin" (Hebrews 4:15). We find the significance and joy of these various trials in Christ's sanctifying work. As we become steadfast through the trials, by His grace, we grow in Christlikeness (sanctification) since He, too, was tempted in every way yet never sinned. The more trials we face and the more varied they are, the more unique opportunities we have to trust in our High Priest, who overcame every temptation and can empower us, through His Spirit, to do the same. For this reason, we can praise God for the big and small trials already faced and those yet to come because every trial brings us one puzzle piece closer to being "perfect and complete."

Perfection in Suffering

> "Now may the God of peace himself sanctify you completely, and may your whole spirit and soul and body be kept blameless at the coming of our Lord Jesus Christ." 1 Thessalonians 5:23

We are not perfect, but that is what God is working toward in us. The completed puzzle is our glorification. That is our hope. It is not our present, but our future, for "hope that is seen is not hope. For who hopes for what he sees? But if we hope for what we do not see, we wait for it with patience" (Romans 8:24-25). Until accomplished, we persevere with patient endurance knowing it is sure. Perseverance is necessary for Christlikeness and, ultimately, our glory in Him.

Like our regeneration and sanctification, our glorification is God's work, too (Romans 8:30). While He commands us to be holy as He is holy (1 Peter 1:15-16), He also empowers us to obey that command as we persevere by His Spirit through our suffering. Sometimes amid the madness and unbearable pain, we would rather go from regeneration straight to glorification; but sandwiched between those two miraculous works is the painful (yet equally miraculous) work of sanctification. We will not be made perfect without testing just like gold will not be purified without fire. Each trial serves its intended good purpose of transforming us piece by piece into the image of Christ. For this reason, we can joyfully receive whatever comes from God's hand and be thankful for it and in it. The trials are part of the purifying process of growing in holiness. When we come out on the other side of each trial, as we submit to the LORD in them, we will come out more like Christ. When we believe these truths, we can better receive God's good gifts which may present as painful trials and tests. As difficult as those gifts may be, we can be sure they are perfect for us because if we receive them with willing hearts and endure them by faith, they will play a vital role in perfecting us.

CHAPTER 30

Weak and Broken Vessels

"But he said to me, 'My grace is sufficient for you, for my power is made perfect in weakness.' Therefore I will boast all the more gladly of my weaknesses, so that the power of Christ may rest upon me." 2 Corinthians 12:9

"A truly humble man is sensible of his natural distance from God; of his dependence on Him; of the insufficiency of his own power and wisdom; and that it is by God's power that he is upheld and provided for, and that he needs God's wisdom to lead and guide him, and His might to enable him to do what he ought to do for Him." Jonathan Edwards[72]

In God's sovereign grace, He uses suffering to ground us while He grows us. The LORD knows our tendency in the flesh to boast of the work He alone accomplishes in us. For this reason, we not only witness His sanctifying work, but we are also able to see our weaknesses at the same time. The humiliation of our pride hurts like few other things, but it is in our confession of weakness that we find His grace and experience His power. We always find the humility of weakness in the grace of sanctification.

We all have weaknesses. The question is whether we will admit them or not. When we're suffering through difficult circumstances and our weaknesses are exposed, it's similar to a boxing match when one fighter hits the other, and while the boxer is down, he hits him again. It's like a hit when we're already down. The realization of our weaknesses is a suffering in and of itself. It hurts our pride, and that's the point. Our pride is the most dangerous threat to

---

[72] Edwards, Jonathan. 1969. *Charity and Its Fruits: Christian Love as Manifested in the Heart and Life.* Banner of Truth.

God's work in us. Self-sufficiency, self-glorification, and self-exultation (all self-focused fear as we revere ourselves) are easy to fall into when things are going well. Even in ministry, when things seem to be clicking right along, we can fall into the trap of self-focused praise.

For the Lord to work in us according to His perfect will, for His will to be done on earth as it is in heaven, we need to be empty vessels, not full of self. Our suffering empties us of ourselves so God can fill us with His Spirit. The apostle Paul understood this truth, and it was this understanding that brought him to a place of boasting in his weaknesses. He knew the power of Christ rests on us when we are weak.

Pride in Self-Sufficiency

> "Not that we are sufficient in ourselves to claim anything as coming from us, but our sufficiency is from God," 2 Corinthians 3:5

Because God knows and loves us, He exposes our weaknesses. The exposure itself doesn't change our hearts, though. The revelation of our weaknesses can harden or break our hearts. A hardened heart, ruled by the flesh, can deny weaknesses and boast in the wrong strengths. This is a common reaction to our exposed weaknesses in a world that takes pride in self-sufficiency, power, and strength. But where we are self-sufficient, we are grace-deficient. Wherever we deny our weaknesses, we deny God's power through His Spirit and His access to rule and reign, suffocating the abundant grace God wants to pour out in each of our lives.

Many scribes and Pharisees, in their self-righteousness, would never admit their weaknesses. They lived in a place of self-sufficiency and "strength" for so long; even being praised as such strong religious leaders by the people, they reached a high position from which they did not want to come down. Their pride hardened their hearts, blinding them to their own weaknesses. It is an easy place we can find ourselves, especially when serving in more public roles. Instead of admitting our weaknesses, we want to deny them under the misguided idea that our efforts are pleasing to God. But there is no fear of the LORD in our self-focused efforts to protect our pride.

As Christians, we want to please God by proving Christ is sufficient. When we suffer or admit that life is hard, we feel we have failed to prove that. But we have misunderstood our suffering. We are not the ones who prove Christ is sufficient; Christ is the One in us who proves that He is sufficient. And He often does that in our suffering. Our suffering exposes our weaknesses, and our weaknesses show that we aren't sufficient. They remind us that apart from Christ, we can do nothing (John 15:5). If we are willing to confess that truth, He does not condemn us for that confession. He receives us with steadfast love and mercy. Christ's sufficiency is not proved by denying our weaknesses but by yielding our broken lives to the Spirit, who works powerfully despite them.

Grace in Brokenness

> "There are some of your graces which would never be discovered if it were not for your trials." Charles Spurgeon[73]

When the Spirit reveals our weaknesses, we don't have to deny them like the Pharisees. We can confess and agree with His revelation. Those who fear the LORD accept that they are weak. Scripture tells us, "With humility comes wisdom" (Proverbs 11:2). Since the fear of the LORD is the beginning of wisdom (Proverbs 9:10), humility is a necessary counterpart to the fear of the LORD. "God opposes the proud but gives grace to the humble" (James 4:6).

Brokenness, or humility, is the catalyst for all good suffering. When we reach the point of brokenness in our suffering, God can work powerfully in that place. Our trials are all intended to bring us to a place of brokenness before God—a place of confession that we are weak but He is strong. David made clear in his psalm, speaking many times of the fear of the LORD, "God is near to the brokenhearted and saves the crushed in spirit" (Psalm 34:18). God is near to us in our brokenness, and He is gracious to save us. Unless we are humble before God because of our insufficiency, we will not know His sufficient grace.

It is a gracious thing when God shows us our weaknesses. Whether He reveals them to us personally or uses others to point them out, He is leading us to a place of brokenness. When the LORD opens our eyes to our weaknesses and humbles us that we might boast in them, even that is His grace. If we were blind to them, we would remain in them. He is showing us the way out of our weakness through His strength. It hurts our pride, but it is a necessary suffering that leads us to the cross. We find the heart of the gospel

---

[73] Spurgeon, Charles. 2000. *Devotional Classics of C. H. Spurgeon*. Sovereign Grace Publishers.

in the Lord's words to Paul, "My grace is sufficient for you, for my power is made perfect in weakness" (2 Corinthians 12:9). God's perfecting work in us follows our acknowledgment of weakness. His power, available to us because of Christ's death and resurrection, is free for all who believe, but it is not for those who think they are strong enough on their own. It is in our humility, confessing our weakness, that God floods us with His grace.

Strength in Weakness

> "For the sake of Christ, then, I am content in weaknesses, insults, hardships, persecutions, and calamities. For when I am weak, then I am strong." 2 Corinthians 12:10

Living in a place of weakness with God, in Christ, is the strongest, most secure place we can be, infinitely better than a place of "strength" without Him. Paul learned this through his suffering. In 2 Corinthians 12, we learn that with divine progress came severe suffering. He received a "thorn in the flesh." This thorn was given to keep him in a place of brokenness and humility before God. While never told what the thorn was, we know it was enough of a burden and strain on Paul that he wanted it gone. He pleaded with the Lord to take it away. It seemed too much for him to bear. It constantly reminded him of his weaknesses, which was God's perfect intention. God wanted to use Paul to glorify Himself, but for Paul to be a willing vessel for God's glory, he needed to be weak enough to rely on God for the power to glorify Himself. We need to know just how weak we are so we will rely on God for His strength.

We think the thorns are the worst thing that can happen to us. As we grow in Christ, our greatest desire is to know Him more, love Him more, glorify Him more—fear Him more. We imagine that means never-ending mountain-top spiritual experiences and impressive Christlikeness at all times. We feel the thorns get in the way of all that we desire to do and be and experience in Christ. But God gives us the thorns to keep us keenly aware of our weaknesses so that Christ can accomplish those deepest desires of our souls.

God knows the hearts of His children and what is best for each one. He gives us our thorns to draw us to Him and reveal Himself to us. Our thorns lead us to the priceless gift we all want: eternal communion with Him. I first heard this poem by Martha Snell Nicholson when my thorns seemed too much, and her words blessed me. She begins by describing herself as a beggar of God standing before Him pleading for a special gift from Him. She continues:

> I took the gift from out His hand, but as I would depart
> I cried, "But Lord this is a thorn and it has pierced my heart.
> This is a strange, a hurtful gift which Thou hast given me."
> He said, "My child, I give good gifts and gave My best to thee."
> I took it home and though at first the cruel thorn hurt sore,
> As long years passed I learned at last to love it more and more.
> I learned He never gives a thorn without this added grace,
> He takes the thorn to pin aside the veil which hides His face.

Jars of Clay

> "But we have this treasure in jars of clay, to show that the surpassing power belongs to God and not to us. We are afflicted in every way, but not crushed; perplexed, but not driven to despair; persecuted, but not forsaken; struck down, but not destroyed; always carrying in the body the death of Jesus, so that the life of Jesus may also be manifested in our bodies." 2 Corinthians 4:7-10

Throughout Paul's second letter to the Corinthians, he encourages them not to lose heart despite their suffering. Even before we learn of his thorn, we hear of many other kinds of suffering he endured. In every case, Paul turns us away from our self-focused fear and back to the hope we have in the gospel through the revelation of "the knowledge of the glory of God in the face of Jesus Christ" (2 Corinthians 4:6). This God-focused fear equips us to endure all the suffering that comes our way because in humility we know the LORD "gives strength to the weary and increases the power of the weak" (Isaiah 40:29).

In our brokenness, our treasure is revealed. Jesus Christ is our treasure, and He puts Himself in us, jars of clay. Clay is a fragile medium—nothing like iron or steel. It is easily breakable. God intended for us to be easily breakable so that we would not become conceited but boast in our weaknesses. When we boast in our weaknesses, we "show that the surpassing power belongs to God and not to us" (2 Corinthians 4:7). In our weaknesses and brokenness, we can display the drastic, yet beautiful contrast God intended for our lives—a glorious work of Christ in weak and broken vessels.

CHAPTER 31

Our Worship as Living Sacrifices

"I appeal to you therefore, brothers, by the mercies of God, to present your bodies as a living sacrifice, holy and acceptable to God, which is your spiritual worship. Do not be conformed to this world, but be transformed by the renewal of your mind, that by testing you may discern what is the will of God, what is good and acceptable and perfect." Romans 12:1-2

"There was a day when I died, utterly died—died to George Müller, his opinions, preferences, tastes, and will; died to the world, its approval or censure; died to the approval or blame even of my brethren and friends—and since then, I have only to show myself approved to God." George Müller[74]

It is the fear of God that compels us to surrender our lives to Him. Through His Spirit, we recognize our sinfulness in light of our holy God, and we understand Christ is the only One who can empower us to do God's good, pleasing, and perfect will. Without the fear of God, we don't understand our inability to live as He calls us. Without the fear of God, we have no care or concern about pleasing Him, so we sense no need to surrender to Him. We live for ourselves and in our own strength. God knows when we live in this fearlessness, even when we don't recognize it ourselves. But God wants to use everything in our lives, including our suffering, to lead us back to the fear of the LORD, opening our eyes to His glory and our desperate need for Him.

Though we were created to worship God, humanity has distorted what that means. We have reduced something so monumental, transcendent, and

---

[74] Pierson, Arthur T. 2000. *George Müller of Bristol: His Life of Prayer and Faith*. Kregel Publications.

glorious to something we can do and explain ourselves. But we can't. In the truest sense, our worship is spiritual worship that must come first from within. And if our worship is to be pleasing to a holy God, it cannot come from ourselves in the flesh, in our own efforts, in our sin. The only way our worship can be pleasing to God is if we give ourselves—our heart, soul, mind, and strength—over to Him so He can change us, accomplishing the holy and pleasing work in us. When we understand that truth, which even this understanding comes from God's grace, we do the only thing that makes sense: we surrender our lives to Him.

Sacrificial Worship Through Surrender

> "And he said to all, 'If anyone would come after me, let him deny himself and take up his cross daily and follow me. For whoever would save his life will lose it, but whoever loses his life for my sake will save it.'" Luke 9:23-24

It's hard to understand the relationship between God's sovereignty and our will, but we don't need to understand it perfectly to know that God gave us commands we fail to obey. Our disobedience proves our will exists. It also proves that, when left to ourselves in the flesh, we would choose to disobey God. When we sacrifice our will in the flesh, which would choose to sin against God, we can submit ourselves to the will of the LORD. The only way we, sinners with no capacity to be holy and pleasing to Him, can obey God, would be to give ourselves to Him.

Surrendering to God is our ultimate path to life in Christ. The more completely we surrender to God, the more we can become like Jesus Christ. The more we die to ourselves in the flesh and deny our own will for His sake, the more His Spirit can live freely in us. When we surrender, not just at one point but each time our will contradicts His, we receive the fullness of God granted to us. He makes Himself visible in us so others can see His love, joy, peace, patience, kindness, goodness, faithfulness, gentleness, and self-control. We willingly give up control and authority of our own lives so that the Master and Author of Life can create the masterpiece He wants to create in us and through us. Even this act of willing surrender does not come from ourselves but by the mercies of God.

Pleasing Worship by God's Mercies

> "It was the mercy of God that gave us Calvary, not Calvary that gave us mercy. If God had not been merciful, there would have been no incarnation, no babe in the manger, no man on a cross, and no empty tomb." A. W. Tozer[75]

Paul brings the first 11 chapters of truth in his letter to the Romans to a fork in the road. He spoke the truth about our sins, the gospel, Jesus Christ, and the greatness of life in Him by His Spirit. What are we going to do about all of God's mercies? There is a necessary application that will prove our understanding of God's mercies. He doesn't ask us to fix our problems or to change our ways. He makes a simple but profound plea that is the ultimate summation of the Christian life: "Present your bodies as living sacrifices."

Bible translations of Romans 12:1 seem to have two meanings from the original text. Some say something relating to "in view of God's mercies" or "on account of God's mercies," while several others say, "by the mercies of God." I have often read this verse thinking of the former meaning even with the latter translation. I think many of us do. We hear Paul's plea that the Romans consider God's mercies as their motivation for surrender. I think that is true and essential. The more we know His mercy toward us, the more willing we will be to surrender our lives to Him, trusting Him to care for us and equip us to do His will. However, the translation "by the mercies of God" leads us deeper still.

The preposition "by" indicates the means of achieving something or "identifying the agent performing the action" (Oxford Language Dictionary). God's mercies are the means through which we can offer our bodies as living sacrifices that are holy and pleasing to Him. We are right to be motivated by His mercies, but it is also because of His mercies that we can be motivated to surrender at all. If it weren't for God's merciful love in sending Jesus to die on the cross for our sins while we were still sinners and rise again so that we might have life in His name, we would not be able to worship Him at all.

---

[75] Tozer, A. W. 2003. *The Attributes of God: A Journey into the Father's Heart.* Christian Publications.

Faithful Worship Because of the Cross

> "I have been crucified with Christ. It is no longer I who live, but Christ who lives in me. And the life I now live in the flesh I live by faith in the Son of God, who loved me and gave himself for me." Galatians 2:20

We can be living sacrifices because of Christ's finished work on the cross. This finished work is His death on the cross *and* His resurrection from the dead. His death cannot eclipse His resurrection because together they are the means through which we can live His life even now, not waiting until heaven. His death is His mercy; His life is His grace.

We don't simply thank Jesus Christ for His sacrifice with words of appreciation. Our worship is more than words. Because He loved us first in this way, we are compelled to live the same surrendered, sacrificial, resurrected, and holy life through His Spirit in us. We show God-focused fear by living as Paul described following his illustration of believers as jars of clay. We are "always carrying in the body the death of Jesus, that that the life of Jesus may also be manifested in our bodies. For we who live are always being given over to death for Jesus's sake, so that the life of Jesus also may be manifested in our mortal flesh" (2 Corinthians 4:10-11).

To carry "in our body the death of Jesus" or to be "given over to death for Jesus's sake" sounds like Paul's same call to offer our bodies as living sacrifices later in Romans. It is not a vain death but a death that leads to life. It is a dying of our own wills and desires in the flesh so that He can accomplish His will in us for the glory of God and the benefit of others. "So that the life of Jesus also may be manifested" communicates two important points:

1. The life of Jesus cannot be in us if we do not carry the death of Jesus in us too. We cannot have all the benefits of His life if we aren't willing to sacrifice our own.
2. The life and death of Christ are to co-exist in the believer's life together, continuously. We are to be living sacrifices (life and death). We show the world His love by dying to ourselves and living in Him.

When we offer our bodies to God as living sacrifices, resisting conformity to the world, by grace because of His mercy, He transforms us. This transformation is from the inside out. It begins with faith when we receive a new heart, which is lived out in our lives for the world to see. It is a visible transformation. The world witnesses the changing of our character as we die more to sin and live more to righteousness (Romans 6). They see the result of the sacrifice of our own will when it contradicts His and an increasing desire to do God's will, no matter the cost. Our death, initially when we become new creations *and* progressively as He transforms us from glory to glory, frees us to live the most abundant and joyful life we could ever live: the life of Christ in us.

Willing Worshipers for His Will

> "For I have come down from heaven, not to do my own will but the will of him who sent me." John 6:38

Presenting our bodies to God is not forced but willingly, just as Christ willingly sacrificed His life for the glory of God and our good. Jesus willingly laid His life down, but not without awareness of the cost. Jesus knew what was ahead, the agony and suffering no one has ever or will ever imagine. He asked God the Father, "if you are willing, take this cup from me; yet not my will, but yours be done" (Luke 22:42). Even though He was weak in His humanity, His Spirit was in perfect submission to the Father, wanting the Father's will above all. In His perfect surrender, God was glorified. It will cost us our lives to be living sacrifices, but when we submit to God, He receives the glory, and His kingdom comes to earth as His perfect will is done (Matthew 6:10).

Doing God's will is the hope and desire of all who fear Him. We know this obedience, motivated by love for Him, is the greatest demonstration of our worship. Though I don't know who said it, this message has stayed with me since I heard it: "I wouldn't so much as pick up a feather if it was not what God wanted me to do." This attitude, "whatever God wants me to do," drives the Christian's heart. It is Christ's heart, His mission, and desire (John 6:38). It is not just our attitude in monumental life decisions but in everyday living. God's people will pick up the feathers when He tells them to or pass them by if He tells them to, with no regard for people's praise or condemnation. At times there will be people yelling in the background telling us to pick up the feather that God commands we leave behind or drop the feather that God has called us to pick up and walk with, but it will not matter to the disciple of Christ who desires to worship Him. Picking up feathers or leaving them behind will be simple, though at times, costly acts of obedience that will give us great joy because we know we are acting as the LORD commands and as He equips. Through our own surrendered lives, we will know more each day the abundant life God means for us comes when we lose our lives for His sake.

There have been several defining moments when God asked me to give up something that meant very much to me. I want to say that I was willing every time, but that would be a lie. In some cases, He graciously brought me to the place of giving it up willingly. In other instances, He painfully stripped me of my longings as I gave up hopes and dreams of what I realized may never be. Sometimes He gave those very things back to me, but other times He didn't, at least not as I imagined them. Looking back at those times, I recognize His sovereign hand at work. Whether I was willing or not, He was still working in my circumstances and in my heart. I have learned many times that God may not want for us what we want, but He will change our hearts in our willing submission. We will find that we want most what He wants for us.

One more note about our willing surrender to the Father's will: Our willingness doesn't always guarantee or spare us from suffering, but our open hand frees the Lord to take from us whatever He needs to take or give to us whatever He needs to give. Understand that our willingness will not affect His sovereignty, but our willingness will affect our attitude of worship when He does what He wills. If we are willing either way, we can worship Him either way.

Worship in the Spirit and the Fear of God

> "'But the hour is coming, and is now here, when the true worshipers will worship the Father in spirit and truth, for the Father is seeking such people to worship him. God is spirit, and those who worship him must worship in spirit and truth.'" John 4:23-24

True worshipers will worship God in spirit and truth. Jesus Christ made it possible for us to worship God in that truest sense. The Living Sacrifice made a way for us to be living sacrifices. Isaiah prophesied about Jesus, describing His character and how He would live. He said, "the Spirit of the LORD shall rest upon him, the Spirit of wisdom and understanding, the Spirit of counsel and might, the Spirit of knowledge and the fear of the LORD. And his delight shall be in the fear of the LORD" (Isaiah 11:2-3).

Isaiah described the Holy Spirit as "the Spirit of knowledge and the fear of the LORD" and Christ's delight was "in the fear of the LORD." This Spirit of the LORD that rested on Christ by direction of the Father is the same Spirit Jesus gave us as our Helper, made possible only through His death and resurrection. Likewise, our knowledge of the truth comes from the Spirit and our delight in the fear of the LORD. I don't think this means that we only delight in fearing the LORD by our actions but also in our communion with God through His Holy Spirit. As Christ delighted "*in* the fear of the LORD", so can we delight *in Christ*, communing with God through His Spirit. The more we surrender ourselves to God, not choosing our way but yielding to His, the more we can join in the holy and pleasing commune with Him through His Spirit and live in the way that pleases Him. All because of Jesus Christ.

Fearing God is not possible apart from the cross of Jesus Christ. It cannot manifest apart from the Spirit of God who dwells in the one who believes in Christ's death and resurrection and what that means for them. No one can give it but the Father of lights through His gracious gift of salvation. The fear of the LORD is inseparable from the Triune God, not just the verbal confession of who He is, but the surrender of our lives to Him now and forevermore. The life surrendered to God is the one that fears the LORD from the inside out.

CONCLUSION

"Since we have these promises, beloved, let us cleanse ourselves from every defilement of body and spirit, bringing holiness to completion in the fear of God." 2 Corinthians 7:1

"Children, Fear God; that is to say, have a holy awe upon your minds to avoid that which is evil, and a strict care to embrace and do that which is good." William Penn[76]

The Christian life doesn't always make sense. It naturally doesn't make sense to the world, but sometimes, it doesn't even make sense to Christians. We must remember that our decision to fear God is not based on our perfect understanding of God's ways but on our perfect God, who understands the best way. He is teaching and growing us up in the fear of the LORD using whatever means necessary so our lives will increasingly demonstrate wisdom, love, and obedience that can only come from Him. By grace He changes His people more into the image of Jesus, purging our sins, making us holy, and always working in the details of our lives for His glory.

God commands us to be holy as He is holy. We try and fail, try and fail, and try and fail. We try, knowing He commands it, but we fail when we make any effort toward holiness on our own. We try to make perfect pound cakes out of our lives, but we often substitute the wrong ingredients and wonder why things don't seem right. As we strive to live purposeful lives, we get too caught up in using convenient substitutes. We may think we are right in using these substitutes, but they could cost us our lives. Jesus Christ is the only One we need, but we need Him to fulfill the good purpose of God in our lives—to

---

[76] Penn, William. 2018. *Fruits of a Father's Love: Being the Advice of William Penn, to His Children, Relating to Their Civil and Religious Conduct.* Forgotten Books.

fear Him, which will lead us to fulfill all the other good purposes He has for us that will bless us and those around us.

As Scripture confirms, the highest purpose for our lives is to fear God, and the visible result of that fulfilled purpose is our holiness. We must connect the fear of God with holiness; they are not unrelated, separate topics. The fear of God is the means by which we become holy; the fear of God will necessarily prove its existence by how we live—with wisdom, love, and obedience to His commands—demonstrated even in suffering, just as gravity proves its existence by its visible effects.

The visible effect of holiness due to the fear of God is not merely external, though. We don't just go around constantly spiritualizing what we do and say because holiness is invisible, Christ in us, before it is visible, His work of sanctification in our lives. God proves His goodness through our lives as we do whatever He calls us to do with excellence for His glory and the benefit of others. A God-fearing life is much deeper and more profound than plugging Bible verses into our conversations or putting crosses on everything as if to prove with trinkets that we fear God. No, goodness in us and the good works that result, for God's sake and by His Spirit, are the overflow of a heart that belongs to God, made holy by the death and resurrection of Jesus Christ.

I pray the Lord has used *Holy Gravity* to encourage and equip you to go into the world aiming to do good, please God, and live holy lives grounded in Christ, attracting many others to Himself. This study has done that for me. When we know whom we serve and consequently fear Him, we cannot do otherwise.

Printed in the USA
CPSIA information can be obtained
at www.ICGtesting.com
LVHW091259211023
761756LV00004B/7